The Debt Generation

The Debt Generation

Written by

David Malone

Edited by

Mark Tanner

LEVEL PRESS

First published in Great Britain in 2010 by:

Level Press Ltd
17 Regent Street
Lancaster
LA1 1SG

A catalogue record for this book is available from the British Library.

ISBN 978-0-9566902-0-3

Prepared and printed by:

York Publishing Services Ltd
64 Hallfield Road
Layerthorpe
York
YO31 7ZQ
Tel: 01904 431213

Website: www.yps-publishing.co.uk

For my grandfather, James Gillis Henry,
and my friend, Henri Goujat,
who both believed a better world was possible.

Contents

About the Author

David Malone is a second-generation documentary filmmaker. His father, Adrian Malone, made the great landmark series including, The Ascent of Man, The Age of Uncertainty, and Cosmos. David's own work includes, Testing God, Soul Searching, and Dangerous Knowledge. He was born in North Shields, grew up around 1970s London and spent nine years in America before joining the BBC. He now works as an independent director, presenter and writer. He is married with three children and lives quietly in North Yorkshire.

David writes at http://golemxiv-credo.blogspot.com

Editor's Note

When I first began to read the original material that forms the basis of this book, I had the same feeling one might get if a close friend were to give you their personal diary to read. I have known David for over seven years, and we have made numerous films together for Channel 4 and the BBC. During this time, we have frequently lived in each other's pockets as we have filmed around Britain, Europe and America. I have also stayed with his family for weeks on end during long, sometimes interminable, weeks of film editing. Despite all this, reading through the material he gave me was a revelation.

In late 2007, before the crisis really got underway, David had managed to convince the BBC to commission a documentary about the possible financial meltdown he was convinced was only months away. Throughout the filming and editing, he would entertain us all with predictions of the doom and gloom to come. 'Lehmans is next, just you wait, September…' Our editor, Stephen, quickly dubbed him Cassandra.

On Friday, September 12, 2008, we finally finished the film. The following Monday, Lehman Brothers declared itself bankrupt and sent the financial world into meltdown. Two days later, our film, High Anxieties – The Mathematics of Chaos, was broadcast on BBC4.

From around the time we started making that film, David began posting comments on the Guardian newspaper's financial web pages. Although we frequently talked about the crisis, I always felt it was a little impolite to read what he was posting – a bit like sneaking a peep at someone's private letters when they are out of the room.

One day, earlier this year, curiosity got the better of me, and I asked David if I could read some of his posts. It was fascinating – a glimpse into the not so private world of someone I thought I knew very well – a real insight into his thoughts, passions and obsessions.

That weekend I went home and downloaded, with his permission, all of his comments from the Guardian website and printed them off. By the time I finished I had a pile of 600 pages. The more I read, the more fascinated I became.

David had made his name directing uncompromisingly intellectual and serious films about the nature of human existence, about God and science. Here was that same intelligence but with a quite different voice – a voice filled with humour, wit, and increasing anger about the injustices being heaped on the many by the rich and powerful.

There was something in his style and tone which felt as if one of the great radicals from the English Revolution, seeing the folly upon which we had embarked, had stepped into the 21st Century desperate to convince us of the error of our ways. It was radical, committed and passionate, but he also had a line of insults of which Jeremy Clarkson would have been proud. Never, in my mind, had doom and gloom been so entertaining.

But it wasn't just the humour. There was a clarity of vision and understanding in his writing which seemed to give him an uncanny ability to see through the fog of confusion and explain the workings of the financial system, not only in the clearest possible way, but also in a way which suddenly made you look at events, and the financial system itself, in a very different light.

It didn't take me long to realise we had the material for what I believed could be a really important book. The question was what type of book?

One option was to take the insights, understanding and analysis David had developed during two years of writing and use them as the basis to write a new history of the crisis – albeit from a different, radical perspective. Step by step, it would carefully take the reader to a new understanding of events with clear signposts along the way showing where we were going. The problem with such an approach, for me, is that it sanitised what I most liked about what David had written: its immediate, visceral quality, which had a power and raw energy, a humour and anger that more contemplative accounts always lack.

If a book was going to work, I believed it needed to keep David's voice with all the anger, insight, vitriol and humour, which make it so distinctive. And that is what I have done.

If you would prefer a calm, considered reflection of events with the benefits and wisdom of hindsight then I am afraid you will be disappointed. These are the historical events as they unfolded in the mind of one man as he tried to convey his thoughts and fears to others. It is history as it happened, driven by events, with all the unexpected turns and twists, lulls and storms.

It is these events that shape the unfolding of the story, but it is from David's reaction to the events that a clear, alternative picture of the crisis emerges. That picture not only clearly challenges all the assumptions and accepted wisdoms we have previously been told, but also points to a very different way forward.

Mark Tanner
Lancaster
September 2010

Author's Note

From the very start of this crisis what concerned me, above all else, was the almost total lack of any real and meaningful debate. Decisions have been made that will affect us for generations to come, but did we ever truly hear competing ideas, explanations and alternative solutions? I certainly didn't. All I heard was a worrying unanimity. Bankers, financial experts, journalists and politicians all repeating each other with the same absolute, shrill, conviction. Only a seemingly endless series of vast bank bailouts, they told us, could avert otherwise certain and catastrophic disaster. It was all far too complicated for the likes of you and me to question what we were not qualified to understand.

Such absolute certainty always gives me cause for thought, so I did what I do in such situations: I began to read – but not economics books. I already knew, from a film I was making at the time, that the assumptions economists used about the real world were fatuous at best. I chose to read what actual traders inside the crisis were saying to each other, day to day, on the message boards where they exchange ideas and information.

Most of what is said on such boards is in trader gibberese, but some of it is a brutally clear analysis of what is happening. I didn't have to agree with their politics to learn from what they had to say. There *was* another view of the crisis. There *were* other ideas of what should be done. Radically different ideas.

The more I read, the stronger my conviction grew that the mainstream media's reporting of the crisis was alarmingly wrong. After three months of reading, I began to write. That was in early 2008. I had no intention of writing a book. I simply felt compelled to voice opposition to the deafening certainties being thrust at me from all sides. What I wrote, under the name GolemXIV, were comments on the Guardian newspaper's website responding to financial news stories.

We had been denied, I argued, a meaningful discussion of the nature of this crisis and the futility of what was being done in the name of fixing it. As the crisis unfolded, I became more and more convinced that what was being done in the name of helping us would instead, whether by design or stupidity, turn us and our children into the Debt Generation: the generation whose principle use and fate would be to pay off other people's debts. It made me angry. Angry at those engineering it, angry at those who justified it, and angry at those who told me there was no alternative.

After nearly two years of commenting on the Guardian, I started my own blog where I still write.

What you have in your hands is a condensation of all that anger, frustration, reading and thinking. My friend and collaborator on many films, Mark Tanner, took everything I had written and formed it into what we hope and believe is a jargon free and readable critique of what, to this day, we are still being told by all the experts, bankers, politicians and journalists.

If, like us, you feel the need to have a different account of our current situation and what we should be doing about it, then I sincerely hope this book offers you something valuable and important.

David Malone
Scarborough
September 2010

Prologue

On July 19, 2007, the Dow Jones average closed the day at its highest point ever.

Three weeks later, on August 9, the huge French Bank PNB Paribas suddenly closed three very large subprime US mortgage funds. The European Central Bank (ECB) was forced to pump €95bn into the market to steady nerves, but the shockwaves had already spread. It wasn't enough. The next day, central banks around the globe were drawn in. The ECB pumped in a further €156bn, the US Federal Reserve, more commonly known as the Fed, put in $43bn and the Bank of Japan a trillion yen – all to try to steady global markets. The markets held their breath.

Five days later, on August 15, the massive US mortgage lender, Country Wide Financial, haemorrhaged 13% of its stock value in a single day. Two weeks after that, on August 31, Ameriquest, the largest specialist subprime lender in the US, collapsed. Then, on September 14, there was a bank run at Northern Rock in the UK amid fears the bank was about to collapse. That day their customers withdrew an estimated £1bn, and the British government had to step in to guarantee all deposits.

These were the warnings that the problem was global and systemic, but nothing of substance was done. Until March 16, 2008, when Bear Stearns imploded.

CHAPTER 1

A Mad Max Future

4 July 08

Many of the brokers and dealers I hear from talk openly of what they are calling a 'Mad Max' future. Bear Stearns was just the harbinger of the storm to come. They think there is a real chance that most of the other big US banks will collapse, with JP Morgan the last to go. They think one of the major bond insurers will go bust despite everything being done to stave off such an 'unthinkable' event. They think we will see an eventual collapse in the dollar. They think there will be a complete meltdown in the bond market. They are talking of Depression 2.0.

I agree with them on all counts.

8 July 08

Ordinary people are still reeling from numbers in the billions. So much so that they just haven't clocked, or just can't absorb, the real numbers waiting in the wings. Enron was small beer compared to what we have to come. When I look at the numbers on the debts I just think of the film The Poseidon Adventure. It's the scene where the captain finally sees the wave rolling towards him. All he says is something like 'God help us' and then the huge ship is rolled over like a bath toy.

The bankers and the über-rich know how high the stakes are. That's why I think it only reasonable to presume that they and their tame politicians will do everything, within and without the law, to head off the collapse of their economic system. Their wealth, positions and power – all they hold dear -depend upon it.

11 July 08

First we had Bear Stearns, now it starts getting serious. Indymac Bank, the California-based mortgage lender, collapsed today. It's the fourth biggest banking failure in US history. They had racked up over $900m in losses. The US regulator, John Reich, of the gloriously titled Office of Thrift Supervision (OTS), said the reason the bank failed was 'due to a liquidity crisis.' A bank goes bust like that, and it's just a liquidity crisis? I don't think so.

A liquidity crisis is when you have lots of money, but in the short-term it's all tied up and you can't lay your hands on it. That's liquidity. If this had simply been a liquidity problem, they had plenty of time to sell some of their assets and get their hands on the money they needed. Why didn't they? Because everyone trading day-to-day knows these assets aren't worth even a fraction of what the banks claim they are worth. They couldn't sell them because nobody would buy them. I don't believe they were just having liquidity problems: they were insolvent.

All the banks are in the same position. When journalists say, 'the banks won't lend to each other', it's at best a half-truth. The real truth is that no bank will accept as collateral any of the assets held by the other banks. They all insist they have valuable assets, yet when they are approached to lend they say, 'Hmm, I don't think your assets are worth what you say they are. You might not be able to pay me back.' They then promptly refuse to lend at all, or if they do, only at a punitive rate of return. That *is* the credit crunch.

It is also the reason they are all so reluctant to bring these assets to market. Their whole claim to solvency depends on everyone believing the assets are worth what they claim. If they had to bring them to market ('mark-to-market' in banker speak) then the real truth would be revealed: their assets are virtually worthless. The market would be like the little boy who told the Emperor he had no clothes. Then it really would be kaput, show over. Arrivaderci Lehmans, Goldman, Merrill, RBS, HBOS, Lloyds et al.

I would not mourn their passing.

15 July 08

The Federal National Mortgage Association, more commonly known as Fannie Mae, and the Federal Home Loan Mortgage Corporation, more commonly known as Freddie Mac, have been teetering on the brink for weeks. If they were to go, the whole system really would blow itself asunder. That's why the secretary of the US Treasury, Henry Paulson, will do everything he can to keep them afloat. Whatever it means, whatever it costs. If they let Fannie and Freddie die, their whole stinking system dies with them.

For those who don't know, Fannie and Freddie are at the heart of what are known as mortgage-backed securities (MBS). These are the assets that are causing all the problems with the banks. They are the reason that Bear Stearns and Indymac went belly up. They are also why a lot of other banks and insurers are going to go the same way.

One particularly useful way of understanding these securities is to see them as a form of private currency used by the banks. It is that currency which is now in crisis.

Official currencies such as euros, pounds and dollars are tied into all sorts of considerations that speculators find restrictive, particularly the desire politicians have for currency stability. The markets neither need nor want stability: speculators need instability to gamble on and make bigger profits. That's why, with the help of Fannie and Freddie, the banks effectively created their own currency, using mortgages to do it.

How do you turn mortgages into a currency? Easy. A mortgage carries the same promise as a dollar bill or a pound note: 'I promise to pay the bearer the sum of …' The only difference is that it's not the government of a country promising to pay the bearer based on future tax revenue. It's someone in America promising to pay their mortgage. Mmmmm.

Sounds dodgy now, but all those involved believed they could spend these bits of paper just like dollars. And they did.

Fannie Mae and Freddie Mac bought up the mortgages from the banks, packaged them up into bundles (securitised them, as it is known in the trade), and then sold them on. The banks and other financial institutions then used this new currency, exchanged it, held it on their balance sheets as good as cash, and speculated with it.

At the start, this 'paper' was backed by solid gold AAA rated mortgages: people who would absolutely be able to pay. But soon the bankers did what every greedy idiot in history has done: they decided to debase the currency so they could print more. They started writing mortgages to people with no hope of ever paying them back. Think of these mortgages as the equivalent of tin. They mixed these tin mortgages into packages with solid gold ones. They then sold the lot on pretending it was all gold.

Nobody worried because in a rising property market even if the debtor couldn't pay back the original loan, the underlying asset, the house, would have gone up in value. Who could lose?

Make loans, don't worry if the debtor can pay you back, then sell them on to Fannie and Freddie who create a new mortgage-backed security. With the money from Fannie and Freddie you can then fund more mortgages. The more mortgages you issue, the more you fuel the property market, the more prices go up, the richer you get until … POP the bubble bursts, people start defaulting, prices fall, and who is left holding lots of bits of paper nowhere near their original value? Why, Fannie and Freddie and all the major banks.

That's the crisis: it's a crisis in the value of the currency used and held by the banks. That is why they are now scrambling to get their hands on our 'real', old-fashioned national currencies. And what do they want to give us in return? You guessed. Their bits of paper they now no longer want.

They chose to mistreat the currency they invented, not us. They now want to suck our currency dry to save theirs. We must not let them.

17 July 08
As this crisis deepens we are going to hear many expert economists and financial advisers telling us what must be done. 'We must' have rates cut by all the central banks. 'We must' get liquidity into the system. 'We must' bail out the banks.

All of these 'we musts' will be underlined by the experts' deep understanding of economics. So, let's ask what it is that these experts understand so deeply. Can we speak of economics as a science?

Well, not in any sense that can seriously be defended. True, it does make predictions. Sadly, none in living memory have ever been right. Not one of the models used by the central banks, treasuries and major traders have predicted any of the shocks and downturns of the last 30 years.

Why is that? Bad luck? Models just need a bit of tinkering? No. They only tell you how the system should act as long as all its key parts and relationships stay the same. But, of course, these things change, and the moment they do is when shocks, downturns, booms and recessions happen. Result? The models never predict anything we need them to predict. They are, for all intents and purposes, virtually useless.

The most amazing thing is that all these economic experts are well aware of all this.

In the end, economics is not a science based on how the real world actually works. It is simply a set of mutually consistent assumptions and rules which make up a self-referencing system. Much like medieval theology or Ptolemaic celestial mechanics.

Ptolemaic celestial mechanics was hugely impressive and scientific looking. Great machines of wheels within wheels and cogs within cogs all designed to model how the planets moved. Immense machines only true experts understood. And the most fantastic thing about it all? It never had any basis in reality! Its predictions were always wrong. It was an elaborate fiction.

I, for one, will have that image in mind when I listen to the shrill orders from expert economists about what must be done.

28 July 08

All the Fed's lending isn't working, and won't work, because it hasn't solved the underlying problem. My granny used to call it throwing good money after bad. Hundreds of billions have been swallowed already and to no great effect other than to postpone disaster long enough for the bankers to get their bonuses. Today Merrill Lynch has just announced $5.7bn write-downs, while Lehmans is hanging by a thread.

The hyper-rich are facing something worse than death: becoming poor. Do you think they will go quietly? I think they will do whatever it takes and sell it to us in the name of saving 'the system'.

We need to remember that we don't need these particular banks for us to survive. If several banks fail, will the world end? No. There are other banks, so the ATM system will still operate. Will you lose your house if your bank goes down? No! Your mortgage will pass to a solvent bank or building society. Will you lose all your money? For the vast majority of people in this country and America their money is safe, not least because it is insured by the government. Those with lots of money will lose lots of it. Pity them.

There is a massive difference between saving a working banking system and saving *these* particular banks. Companies go out of business everyday – it is a fact of life in a market economy. Administrators go in, and the businesses are wound down in an orderly fashion. The same could happen with the banks. When a bank goes under, its shareholders lose everything, then it's the bondholders turn. Those who lent the bank money lose it. In the good times, the shareholders and bondholders were happy to take their share of the profit knowing what the risks were. Now there are losses, they have a legal and moral duty to take their share of those as well.

Ordinary depositors, like you and me, won't lose out. We would still have access to our accounts up to the limit of the government guarantee. That guarantee means the government has a legal obligation to ensure *we* don't lose out, even if the bank collapses. We should also realise that, even in a collapsed bank, there will still be valuable assets. These assets can, and should, be first used to protect the depositors, and then the taxpayer. Until that is done, they shouldn't be used to settle the banks' other debts.

While all this is happening, other solvent banks would still be functioning which we could move to. New ones would be set up. I am not pretending that a number of bank failures would be a walk in the park, but we shouldn't believe the nightmare scenarios being painted by the banking elite. It is a nightmare for them; it doesn't have to be for us. *We* would be able to get through the very short-term, acute crisis caused by the failure of a number of banks. The alternative is to be blackmailed into having the super-rich be too wealthy to be allowed to fail. If that happens, *we* will be paying off *their* debts for a generation to come.

Look at it this way. A man walks into a bank and says, 'I have immediate, crippling debts which I cannot possibly pay off, so please lend me the money to keep me in business and pay my debts.'

The bank manager asks what collateral the man has. The man replies that although he has many assets he can't sell them at the moment because no one wants them, and so he can't get a fair price for them.

The manager starts to suspect a chancer. 'A fair price is what someone will pay you for them at the time you need to sell,' he explains. 'That's rule number one.' The man starts to panic. 'It's an emergency. Lend me the money NOW, and I'll pay you back out of the profits of my business and from selling my assets when they recover their worth.'

The manager is a tolerant fellow and asks to look at the man's business model. When he looks he nearly faints. The man is truly, deeply in debt. His assets are so putrid that many of them will never recover any value. He is also leveraged to insane levels. His exposure to future losses is so high that he has almost no chance of ever becoming solvent, even with the loan he is asking for.

The manager is so amazed he indulges his own curiosity. 'How much do you need?' he asks. The figure the man asks for is so large the bank doesn't actually have enough itself. The man is unmoved. 'I suggest *you* borrow the money to lend to *me*', he says to the bank manager.

The manager is amazed at the brass neck of the man and asks, 'If we do borrow the money, who will pay the interest? You?'

'Oh no,' says the man. 'That's your business! *You* pay your own interest.'

'Let me see if I've got this straight', said the manager. 'You want *me* to go into crippling debt and for *me* to pay all the interest on this debt so that *I* can give *you* money to pay off *your* insane debts and allow *you* to run a failed business model of insane leverage. Why the hell should I?'

At which the man pulls out a gun and holds it to his own head and says, 'Because *I* am too important to be allowed to fail.'

We mustn't be so stupid as to believe this.

29 July 08

There are strong rumours of an imminent collapse of one of the big US banks. It looks like Lehmans is about to go. It will go for the same reasons that Bear Stearns went. Bear Stearns didn't go because it 'couldn't get loans to cover its business' as some commentators suggested. That's as daft as saying someone died of a fever. True, as far as it goes. But what the person really died of was the disease that was causing the fever. Not getting loans is the fever, but the disease that was stopping them from getting the loans is what you want to identify. Bear Stearns couldn't get loans because too many of their assets were worthless. The same was true for IndyMac.

That's why they won't be the last. Many of the assets held by the other banks are similarly worthless. Lehmans is likely to be next over there, HBOS, RBS and Alliance & Leicester over here.

The main problem is that our governments have allowed the banks to value these so-called 'assets' themselves. Typically, they are being shown at very near their full face value – the value they had when they were created. The banks do this by what they grandly call 'mark-to-model'. This means they refer to a computer model they themselves have built which will, they say, estimate what the asset should be worth if the market were functioning well. There is an elaborate theory for this, but it was never anything but a sham dressed up in jargon with a generous dash of hokum. Lots of words to basically say, 'we'll set whatever price we like the sound of.' They then call the asset a 'level three asset' and file it on their accounts at the value they have chosen. This is why, in the midst of this crisis, they are claiming to be perfectly solvent and well-capitalised. Believe at your peril.

The other way of valuing these assets, which the banks *don't* like, is called mark-to-market. This means letting the market decide. Bring out your assets, and let's look at them in the clear light of day to see who wants to buy. When it comes to everyone else, the bankers are usually rabidly keen on this free market solution. It's not, however, something they particularly like for themselves.

The fact of the matter is that when their assets are forced into the market, miracle of miracles, they do find a price and a buyer. The only problem is that the price is too low for the bankers' tastes: 26 cents on the dollar recently for typical debt-backed paper. Such reality is far too ghastly for the bankers, who lobbied to suspend mark-to-market and use their preferred mark-to-model.

We mustn't allow them to get away with this ridiculous charade. We need to force *all* the so-called level three assets and bad loans into the market to see what they are really worth.

I am not talking about retrospectively altering the laws or breaching anyone's legal or human rights. I am simply talking about forcing those who made deals to face the consequences. Like it says in the small print: 'The value of your asset may go down as well as up.' Welcome to the party!

A long chain gang of the greedy and the reckless will pull each other into the abyss, one after another, all chained together by their stupidity and debt. And so it should be.

2 Aug 08
Lloyds TSB profits have just dived 70% because of write-downs, and Alliance & Leicester have announced an even bigger fall of 99%!

Unbelievably, there are still people out there, including Ben Bernanke, the head of the Fed, and Henry Paulson, the secretary of the US Treasury, talking about this as a purely subprime crisis. This is *not* a subprime crisis. That is like identifying the clod of earth that started a landslide and saying, 'It's the clod of earth crisis.' Yes, it certainly was what started the whole thing, but the crisis, the landslide, is made up of a whole lot more than the clod that started it.

If this crisis were just about subprime loans, then enough money has been pumped in to settle most of those bad debts. But the problem was never just those loans. The real problem is far, far larger than the total value of all those defaulted home loans put together.

The real crisis is because the banks and brokers fed those now worthless mortgage-backed debts into a vastly unstable, upside-down pyramid of debt-fuelled speculation. First they turned the loans into securities, and then on top of the securities they created derivatives. If you imagine owning a security as being like owning a racehorse, then owning a derivative is more like betting on that horse. There are only so many horses to own, but anyone and everyone can place a bet on them. The creation of derivatives effectively opened up a global betting shop where you could place all manner of exotic bets, from the future worth of other people's assets to the future value of whole exchanges. You can even write derivatives on derivatives, bets on other bets, and write as many as you want as often as you want.

The paper value of those debts is in the trillions. How the hell did some poor bloke in America wreck it all by not paying his mortgage? The same way as a clod of earth can start a landslide. If the whole thing is unstable, it only takes one pebble to come loose for the whole lot to come crashing down.

6 Aug 08

Bloomberg just announced that American International Group (AIG) is upping its loss from credit default swaps (CDS) for the second quarter to $14.7bn, making a total loss of $26.2 billion. That's in just three months!

If AIG were to go, they would bring everyone down with them because they are the ones at the very centre of the credit default swap market. This is now worth over $50 TRILLION – four times what the whole US economy produces in a whole year.

Credit defaults are great. They are a form of guarantee or insurance for all sorts of debt. If you want to buy a mortgage-backed or debt-backed piece of paper but think the claims that it is all AAA and yummy good are slightly Chinese powdered milk, then you can see me, your friendly neighbourhood credit default swap merchant. I'll insure the stuff you've bought against any remote possibility that it might default.

If it defaults, I will pay out. That's what insurance is for: you pay me a premium up front, I take the risk. Your paper is now insured against default, making it AAA (via insurance), while I get rich from all the premiums. I, of course, want to get richer, so I write the same insurance for everyone who will do business with me. As long as the market goes up, we can all get stinking rich and laugh at the poor people.

Now, of course, I don't have that much actual money to cover everything I have insured. But, fabulously, I bought one of those nifty risk models, and lo! my model tells me that the chance of a lot of the debts defaulting at the same time is tiny. With as little as $80 million I can insure $3 or $4 billion of swaps. Lots of people did. Have another bottle of Bolly! I'm going to.

Now, just in case disaster should come to pass, I cover myself by making another agreement with someone else, effectively insuring myself. The traders like to call this spreading the risk. In fact, the result is long chains of people all linked to each other. I take on a liability with my left hand but try to pass on the risk with another agreement on my right. The fellow to my right does the same. The system has become so complex and interwoven that the last person in the chain will often be someone who appears earlier in the chain as well. No one has the faintest idea where the buck stops. In the good times, no one bothers; in bad times, it's quite a different story. It's like a nuclear chain reaction.

Someone has a defaulting loan. You insured that loan, so they ask you to pay up to cover the default. You pay them and in turn seek money from those who took swaps from you. As soon as one person in the chain starts having trouble paying, the reaction spreads … and spreads. They can't pay you, so you can't pay the person you owe, who in turn can't pay the person they owe. And so it goes, one bankruptcy after another. Try it at home with a line of dominoes. It's much safer.

AIG is at the very centre of all this. They have $450bn in credit default swap contracts. Once they start having to pay out, which they are now having to do, they will quickly run out of money. They simply can't cover all their liabilities because they are far too highly leveraged. Once they run out of money, all those they owe are in deep trouble, and so the reaction will spread.

This is what people mean by 'systemic risk'. In short, AIG is going to go under, and when it does it will drag lots of banks and hedge funds with them. Enjoy!

13 Aug 08

Some people say the Fed might have to bail out all the US bank collapses and end up effectively making the taxpayer take on all their worthless, toxic debts. My question is can it? It simply doesn't have that kind of money. They would have to borrow. But could anyone borrow the amount needed? I seriously wonder if the US national debt rating could take it. Just trying to underpin AIG on its own could see the rating agencies downgrade US national debt.

Of course, they could always print new money, but then what would happen to the value of the dollar? I can't see any alternative to devaluation and inflation going into orbit.

So far, the Fed has done nothing to substantially affect the total money supply, but once they start to print and pump new money into the system the whole thing changes. The value of the money ordinary people use to buy their food starts to slide. I don't think that day is far off now. There's a line of institutions waiting their turn to go belly up. The market players know who they are. Hell, some of *us* know, and we're little people.

These are dangerous times.

17 Aug 08

At the moment, people's fear is still mixed with enjoying watching the super-rich bleat, but when the financial crisis truly spreads to the real economy that's when ordinary people will suddenly get it and feel the effects. When they get laid off and the price of food doubles, then it'll be a different story. That's where your street protests and riots will come from. I don't believe we are far away from this.

Because of the way the system has evolved it only takes a small 1 or 2% decline in profits to bring the whole thing crashing down. How? Easy. Once upon a time, growth was paid for by actual profits based on an actual increase in productive capacity. You made more, sold more and then used your greater profits to fund more growth. Capitalism for Beginners, course 101.

Then, ten years or so ago, a new trend matured called leveraged growth. With this you didn't need actual profits to fund future growth but simply the *promise* of future profits. This was nothing new: what was new was the extent of it.

Instead of waiting for actual profits, growth was funded by borrowing – by taking on debt. It's a great game once you start because promises of future growth can be increased as much as you wish. They can also be rolled over further and further into the future. While it works it's magic because the more the more leveraged you become, the more you can grow.

If, for example, I want to start a construction company, I might take out a loan (issue debt) to build some houses. Each of these houses holds out the promise of profit in the future if growth continues and prices rise. On the basis of this future growth, I take out more loans (issue more debt) to build more houses. All the time, this is dependent on some growth being shown to underpin the increasingly enormous promise of even more profits in the future. In no time at all, I am able to tell my friends I am a millionaire. My company then issues debt for millions more. I buy lots of Bolly and quickly move into a big house with my new, perfectly tanned wife who confesses she only married me because I am so highly leveraged.

If this all seems like a house of cards, that's because it is. Let's call it the Financial House of Cards. It is as if, and I thank Karl Denninger for this analogy, a man who had £10 took out a loan for £100 and then showed that he had made a profit and was richer by £100. Sure, there is more money in his account, but he is actually poorer because he owes the £100, plus the interest on the loan. He can, however, keep up the illusion of wealth as long as his bank has faith in him and allows him to roll his debt forward indefinitely. But the day his bank gets a little spooked and calls the money in – SPLAT – he's bust.

Or think of it another way. Imagine buying a house for £100k. You put down a £3k deposit, your equity in the house. You are leveraged, as they say in the business, at roughly 33:1. For every £1 you have invested you owe nearly 33. Now, if prices rise by just 3% in a year you have doubled your equity. Good for you. But if they fall by just 3% your equity is completely wiped out. That's how just a very small fall of 2-3% can completely wipe out the capital of those who are highly leveraged.

Leverage is, to mix metaphors rather horribly, like gearing. It amplifies the power of the capital you start with but, just like gears, it also works in reverse. When the gains turn to losses they come faster and are bigger and more difficult to stop.

Everyone played this game including governments, banks and a lot of big corporations. The use of leverage and debt-as-assets was like steroids. Those who used it grew impossibly huge, impossibly fast. It made them aggressive and blind to the risks. Anyone who tried to play clean got beaten up and bought out. Now, however, as the crisis bites, those who did use it are going to quickly start discovering the downside: if you live by leverage, you die by leverage.

That's why we are going to start seeing signs of the crisis hitting the 'real economy' very soon. Corporations like General Motors (GM) are going to go bust precisely because they are so highly leveraged. In this climate, no one will roll over the insane debt levels that were routinely being rolled over during the bubble years.

And it's all linked. When General Motors and Chrysler lay off thousands of workers, those are the next people who will start defaulting on their mortgages. That means more write-downs for the banks holding the mortgages and mortgage-backed securities.

And then we mustn't forget the whole credit default swap mess. Credit defaults swaps weren't just written on mortgage-backed securities. They were also written on corporate debt to insure against possible default. General Motors and General Electric (GE), for example, have billions of swaps written on their debt.

The most fantastic thing with credit default swaps is that they are almost totally unregulated. Virtually anyone can buy them and lots of people did. You don't even have to be the creditor. This means if companies like General Motors do start defaulting on their loans, no one knows who will end up having to pay out. Maybe they don't know themselves. Maybe they know but won't say. It doesn't matter really. What does matter is that they are all absolutely terrified of the possible exposures to huge losses they could each incur.

Future perfect? I don't think so.

21 Aug 08

You look at what has been happening in the last weeks and still there are journalists saying, 'Oh, it's just a liquidity problem – nothing wrong with the fundamentals – therefore we will only have a few quarters of downturn. Nothing that some aggressive cuts in interest rates and lots of loans from the Fed won't sort out.'

Haven't they being paying any attention at all?

Do they know what a debt-backed asset is? Do they understand why they are trading at a few cents on the dollar and many at zero? Do they know why the banks are hiding a mountain of them in what they call level three assets? Do they know why this is even important?

Do they understand what will happen if, or more likely when, AIG gurgles its way under the water?

Do they understand that the US may have to bail out General Motors and Ford not because they have any prospect of becoming profitable anytime soon, but because if they went bankrupt no one knows how vast a meltdown it would precipitate in the credit default swap market?

Do they know how large the possible losses in that market are? Do they understand why this makes our bailout packages so laughable and sad?

Do they know that the cost of insuring even US and UK sovereign debt is now starting to go up because they are pricing in a significant chance of national defaults?

Do they realise this may mean that once we have funded the bailouts, it is very unlikely we will be able to fund any kind of social programmes to help those people who are going to be pole-axed in 2009?

Did they stop to think that because of this crisis no governments are going to take any meaningful action to avert the even larger crisis that is waiting for us called climate change?

One thing is certain: a normal recession this isn't. If you have a liquidity problem, you get four to six quarters of downturn. It takes that long to work it through the system. But since it's actually a solvency problem, talk of four to six quarters of recession is just whistling in the dark to keep your spirits up.

Those talking Depression 2.0 are much nearer the mark.

The financial crisis will get much, much worse before it gets better. We are then going to see the real economy severely hit, with unemployment rocketing. We will also see rising inflation, with food shortages in poor countries and food too expensive for the poor to afford in rich countries like America. In such a situation, those holding power will feel justified in taking whatever actions they think necessary to 'maintain order'.

Act one of this crisis has been financial. Settle down folks, the lights are going down and the curtain is about to go up on act two. I promise it will be full of enough blood and drama to keep us groundlings spellbound.

CHAPTER 2

A Hole in the Ice

30 Aug 08

Alistair Darling finally said what quite a few people have known for a while. 'Britain', he revealed, 'is facing arguably the worst downturn in 60 years,' cheerfully adding a little later, 'and I think it's going to be more profound and long-lasting than people thought.'

Just a few facts for Mr Darling to consider:

All the damage so far has been due to subprime mortgages, but now two other insanely unwise and unstable types of US mortgages are going to go boom: ALT-A and Option ARM. The total lent on these two kinds of mortgages together may be even larger than the whole subprime pool. As they begin to default, more of the mortgage-backed securities and derivatives the banks hold on them will have to be downgraded and more, lots more, write-downs will have to be announced.

The banks know this. That is why, despite the billions already thrown at them, they are still not lending to each other. And the problems aren't just with the banks. In the States, the Federal Deposit Insurance Corporation (FDIC), which settles the affairs and debts of banks that fail, has already used up a huge part of its total reserves dealing with the fallout from just the few banks that have gone under so far. There are over a hundred more banks on the danger list. The FDIC simply doesn't have the money to deal with them all, and they know it. What will happen then?

If all that isn't enough, let's factor in Fannie Mae, Freddie Mac and AIG. All three of them are on the very brink of collapse, and if just one goes, the whole system could go with them.

Alistair Darling didn't tell the whole truth: he just told a tiny little bit more of it than the rest of the financial world.

5 Sept 08
US unemployment shot up last month to its highest level in five years. This apparently caught some commentators by surprise. We are on the verge of Depression 2.0 and these people are 'surprised' that unemployment went up? Planet Earth calling! Planet Earth calling! Can you hear me? Hello!

8 Sept 08
Take a deep breath ... and another ... EIGHT HUNDRED BILLION DOLLARS. That is what the US government has just put in the pot to save Fannie and Freddie, and it won't be enough. It will keep them afloat for a while, but the losses are going to keep coming. They have $5.3 TRILLION lent or underwritten in outstanding mortgages, so if Henry Paulson, the secretary of the US Treasury, thinks this is the last time he is going to have to slip his hand in the American purse to bail them out, he is, sadly, very mistaken. As this crisis gets worse, their debts will increase in billions by the day. $850bn simply won't do the trick.

10 Sept 08

What is the argument that chief chimp Bush and his gang of neo-con cowboys have just trotted out for spending these billions nationalising Fannie and Freddie rather than letting their beloved free market sort things out? That the institutions are 'too big to fail.' That's like saying you can't cut out a cancer because too much of your life blood is flowing through it. It's a cancer! You don't cure a cancer by 'having confidence in it.' Only a coward nurtures the cancer that is sucking him dry.

The longer the authorities let this cancer survive, the more it spreads. The more it spreads, the worse things are going to become. Despite all our billions, the end will be the same.

The problem is the virtually worthless assets rotting away in the banks' vaults. Because the mortgage-backed securities consist of lots and lots of different mortgages sliced and diced together, each time a mortgage defaults the stream of money coming in to the owner of that security reduces. When lots of mortgages default this causes the money coming in to drop dramatically. This is how mortgage-backed securities become 'toxic'. You paid a lot for the original security, but the cash flow has now reduced to a trickle. That is why no one wants to buy it from you, at least not at a price that helps you.

The problem, at the root of this crisis, is that the banks are still claiming the full face value for these assets. This is despite the fact that they couldn't get anywhere near this price on the open market.

What we really need is for all these assets and debased paper IOUs held by the banks to be brought onto the open market to find their true value. Surely nothing heretical there Mr President? There must be no more talk of 'impaired markets', 'level three assets' and other econocrap mumbo-jumbo. As long as the banks are allowed to decide for themselves what these assets are worth, there can be no solution to this crisis. Let's look at them in the clear light of day and see what they are really worth.

What we must NOT do is bail out the banks' hyper-inflated mortgage-backed currency with our own good currencies of dollars, euros and pounds. If we do, we risk giving ourselves, and future generations, debts that will cripple us for decades. They will be rich, with our good currencies, and we will be left holding their worthless bits of paper. We need to clear the bad debts from the system, and the sooner we do it the better.

The fact is that the losses are going to be taken by someone at some point no matter what. No amount of sprinkling fairy dust and empty rhetoric can make them go away. Clearing the debts now won't be nice, in that losses would be taken that are currently being hidden away, but the advantage is that the losses would be taken by those who should take them instead of passing them on to a whole generation of taxpayers.

There is no pain free way out of this. It's the banks that made the losses, so let them, not us, pay for it. All we need is courage.

15 Sept 08

Sitting calmly? Good … Lehman Brothers went this morning … deep breaths … in … out.

Now relax for a minute, because amid the mayhem and panic there's a really interesting question to be asked. If, back in March, Bear Stearns was too big to be allowed to fail because 'it might trigger a systemic failure', then why isn't that true of a much bigger bank like Lehmans?

It is true, of course. Lehmans might trigger a systemic failure. It's just I'm not sure either the Fed or the US Treasury can afford to save them. And that is the real story. The Fed simply doesn't have the money. It is running out fast and will soon be bankrupt itself and have to go to the Treasury for a hand out.

So what about the mighty US Treasury? Surely they can save anyone and everyone? Actually no. After putting $850bn into the pot to save Fannie and Freddie even the US Treasury cannot help now. Any more bailouts and they risk an even more mind boggling problem: the international bond market refusing to buy any more US national debt in the form of US treasury bonds.

The idea used to be that no loan could be as safe as lending to the US Treasury. They couldn't ever default, could they? Well, some in the bond market are already beginning to worry that, yes, the US Treasury could default. Is this why they have had to let Lehmans go to the wall, and why they will have to let others go as well? If they hadn't let them go, they would have run the truly cataclysmic risk of the international bond market refusing to fund America any more. Then what?

If the bond market ceases to believe America can and will honour its debts – which are truly staggering already – then the US government are left with only two choices when the municipalities start to beg for money to pay for local services. Either the government starts to print money and start inflation, or they say no to the hungry and homeless people of America. That is the nightmare that is keeping the US authorities up at night.

17 Sept 08

$80bn was given to AIG yesterday to save them going under. Now it becomes clear exactly why they couldn't afford to bail out Lehmans.

At exactly the time Lehmans was going down so was AIG – the lynch pin of US credit defaults. Lehmans was heavily exposed to credit default swaps, but nothing compared to AIG. I think the US Treasury couldn't afford to save both. They chose AIG. That is a measure of how much more important the insurance of the debt is over the debt itself. The insurance is the veneer of respectability plated on to the tin beneath. Take it away, and the nakedness of every banks' assets are exposed. That's why they saved AIG.

If the players had felt sure AIG would be safe, they might have considered trying to save Lehmans, but at that moment, no chance. The sad and ugly truth is that AIG is not saved. AIG is getting sicker, not better. In fact, I think it is still in very great danger of going down. They are still sucking in vast new injections every time a new liability shows up. Wait till GMAC, the company that provides the financing for most General Motors' car dealers, goes under next week. That will create another ripple of credit default settlements and spell more trouble for AIG. They know this. When AIG eventually does go under it will cause a credit default swap chain reaction that will make the fall of Lehman Brothers look like a sparkler at a children's party.

18 Sept 08

The cancer is spreading. HBOS shares have just collapsed. Ask yourself this: who had enough shares in HBOS that they could sell them in sufficient numbers to collapse a bank?

Was it a) lots of small shareholders or b) hedge and other funds selling and shorting the hell out of the market to stave off their own demise? (HBOS being merely the collateral damage.)

This isn't over. The stock collapses are, in part, because the banks are all over-leveraged and sitting on a mound of worthless assets. But they are also happening because there are still City boys and girls speculating to save their bonuses who care not a pin nor a fart about the rest of us.

Next will be Morgan Stanley, then Washington Mutual, then lots of regional banks in the States, then the commercial real estate and car loan sector. Expect GMAC to collapse and GE's financial arm (GE Capital) to go as well.

City boys and girls speculating in order to make themselves rich got us into this mess, and they won't stop until they have buried us all

20 Sept 08

Mr Paulson and the other smart guys at the US Treasury have just come up with a plan to solve all our problems. They have called it the Troubled Asset Relief Program (TARP). It requires spending at least $700bn of taxpayers' money buying up the bad debts and toxic assets held by the big banks. If the plan goes ahead then it will, I believe, be part of the largest and most flagrant redistribution of wealth from ordinary people to the rich in the history of humankind.

Under the plan, ordinary Americans will get to pay the debts of immensely rich and greedy people who owe money to other immensely rich and greedy people so that they can all carry on being immensely rich and greedy. God forbid that any of them should be made to suffer the consequences of their actions. Nice job Mr Paulson.

And where exactly is all that money coming from anyway? There isn't a government in the West, not even the US

Treasury, which has a pile of money that big just sitting there. Paulson will have to borrow it from the international bond market and use future taxes to pay it back. The rich will be relieved of their debts, and we will be indentured to the institutions that they own. *We* will owe *them*. Taxes on *our* labour and *our* children's future labour will be used to pay off *their* debts for years to come.

At the moment, because the bankers and their friends are still posturing as the 'experts', they are presenting this solution as the only solution. It isn't. They are also pretending that what they are protecting is the 'free market'. They aren't. What they have created and are protecting is the most manipulated, intervened in and unfree market anyone has ever seen. Both their expertise and their 'free market' plan are a lie. We don't have to become enslaved and frightened into taking on their debts. They made the shit sandwich; they should eat their share – a large share – I insist.

Whatever happens, we must not let this lunacy be foisted upon us here in Europe. The American people should reject it. We must not head down this road.

26 Sept 08
Another one bites the dust. Paulson's plan came too late to save Washington Mutual. $188bn in deposits and still they went down to have their carcass picked over by the vultures at JP Morgan Chase. It won't be the last. This is far from over. Even if Paulson's plan gets passed by Congress, the debts are simply too large, the assets too putrid, for them to do anything but delay the inevitable.

3 Oct 08
After a couple of major hiccups, and some thinly veiled claims that the end of civilisation was at stake, Paulson's plan to buy

up the banks' toxic assets, the TARP, was finally approved by the House of Representatives.

Let's be clear. The only way the American taxpayer doesn't get shafted by this plan is if the assets are bought at, or near, the present market value. The problem for the banks is that if they are forced to sell at near market value then it doesn't help them at all and they fail. Given this conflict of interests, guess who's most likely to get screwed?

Then there's the small problem of how to pay for it. Either the US Treasury goes to the bond market or they print. For the bond market route to work the US government has to guarantee that the bonds will be honoured no matter what. No matter what social unrest unfolds, no matter what a future Congress might decide – the bond market has to be convinced their bonds will be repaid.

If this happens, there will be NO money at all for welfare or medical or education programmes. When people vote for Obama, presuming change will happen, and then find all those hopes are dashed because all the money went to the bankers, I think you'll see widespread riots throughout the US.

If they decide to print, rather than borrow, they may temporarily solve the US debt problem, but they would screw all those countries holding US bonds as the value of those bonds would be inflated away. China, for one, won't be happy.

Any way you cut it, it is going to end badly. And that's even before you ask whether a mere $700bn will work given the real levels of bad debt out there. I think the answer is rather clearly, no, it won't work. I am of the opinion that the time has come to stop listening to the assurances of our political leaders and start thinking instead of what we need to do to survive Depression 2.0 which is very nearly upon us.

4 Oct 08

Quite incredibly, there are some people saying that all this money being used to buy up the banks' dodgy assets could actually be a 'good investment'. The reason they give? Although the 'assets' are virtually worthless at the moment, 'when the economy picks up the value will return.' So, in the meantime, we must protect those banks owing vast sums and pay their debts for them in the hope that in some faraway future we can recoup our money?

Look at it this way. I have a half-empty biro on my desk. Today it's virtually worthless, but one day in the future it may become a valuable museum piece. So, can I claim now that it is valuable? Would you, Mr Banker, want to pay me today what it *might* be worth when it becomes an antique? You personally? No? Then why should an entire tax paying nation do that for you and your vault of scrap paper?

Plus, there is the trifling point of whether you believe the value of some of these assets will ever return. A huge amount of the paper isn't valued directly by some house waiting for property prices to go up. Most of it is highly structured and many times removed from anything of real use value. Once they started creating derivatives and betting on anything and everything, that direct connection with real world value was lost.

And how does value return to the trillions in credit default swaps? It doesn't, does it? If you are owed money from insurance on a defaulted loan, but the company who owes you the insurance has gone bankrupt, you can wave your bit of credit default swap paper around all you like, but however long you wait it is not going to magically turn into a million dollars.

In short, I don't want to wait for the value of the banks' worthless assets to return and be on the hook until they do.

Not least, because I see no reason at all to believe the value will return. Let them wait if they want to, but please tell them to keep their hands out of my pocket while they do.

7 Oct 08

Not to be outdone by the Yanks, Gordon Brown has just announced a 'bold and far-reaching solution to the crisis' that will, he claims, 'help every family and business in the country.' Gordon's plan? Essentially provide £500bn for the banks!

Gordon's hope is that flush with our money the banks will start lending to each other and to businesses urgently in need of cash. Fat chance of that Gordon! Banking and money markets have seized up because the banks don't have any real money – money that people believe is actually worth something. All they have is lots of paper. They will use *our* money to cover *their* debts to stave off *their* bankruptcy. That's what matters to them: their own survival, sod everyone else.

Look at what the moneymen do Gordon, not what they say. Are the banks trusting each other's assurances that they only have a 'temporary liquidity' problem and are otherwise solvent, well-capitalised and on the mend with a view to it all being over by Christmas? No.

Investment is about confidence and trust. Those things are, in many ways, more valuable commodities than houses and promissory notes. The bankers and brokers have bankrupted themselves of both these commodities. That's the ironic part of it. No one believes them. Hell, they don't even believe or trust each other. So what kind of fool would listen to them?

The only bit of the 'plan' that will create a trickle of lending is the proposal for the Bank of England to underwrite £250bn of new loans. This should prompt the banks into some lending because we, not them, are on the hook if it isn't paid back. Should the loan default there will be no recourse, no repayment, nothing in return for us. More than two years budget for the entire NHS paid to the banks and gone.

Fantastic work Gordon. I thank you; my children thank you too.

8 Oct 08

Let's watch the bond markets tomorrow. Have you seen what is happening to yields and sales of long-term US treasuries? They can't sell the longer-term ones. What the market wants to buy is one and two-year. My guess is that the credit default swaps mess will spook the bond market even more. There is every chance it is going to start drying up soon. When it does, where do you think the US Treasury or the Bank of England is going to get all this promised bailout money? Who will buy their bonds? Bear in mind when the bond market stalls that isn't called a recession: it's called a depression. At least it was the last time.

The only other route is to print, but printing gets you Weimar Germany and Zimbabwe. See what a great plan our experts have cooked up.

9 Oct 08

Yesterday the US had to bail out AIG, again. $85bn the first time was not enough. Yesterday they had to find them another $37.8bn. Notice the exact amount. What that suggests (thanks to Karl Denninger for pointing this out) is that this was to cover a specific liability, which means it's not going to be the last. There are still trillions in credit defaults waiting out there. Trillions.

AIG is sinking and the US can't save it. If they could, they would have already.

Imagine we are all living on an ice sheet that a small group of men are walking across. They are roped together for safety, or as the financial world characterizes it: to spread the risk. Great in theory, but each man is carrying an anvil of debt. Each is so convinced that one day their anvil of debt will turn to gold that they refuse to put them down. One, let's call him Lehman, falls through a hole in the ice. The ropes tighten; everybody stops still. No one can move.

What the rest of us living on the ice should do is make them put down their anvils, and let them slip down the hole Lehman made. There would be huge losses, many of the men wouldn't make it back, but the ice the rest of us are living on would be safe, the hole wouldn't widen. But we are not doing this. Instead we are walking out carrying our own anvils of debt to help them. As the hole gets bigger and bigger the entire ice sheet threatens to crash

10 Oct 08

The International Monetary Fund (IMF) has just released a report saying that next year Britain will suffer a full year of recession. Only a year? Are you kidding me? How can they peddle such palpable nonsense?

The IMF is perhaps the most spectacularly, ideologically blind institution to have been inflicted upon people since the Inquisition. In fact, they have much in common. Like the Inquisition, the IMF is ruled absolutely, by ideologues who would rather we all burned in hell than admit their particular, distorted version of the 'free market' is wrong. They have a consistent history of insisting on economic measures that have done long-term damage to almost every country they have got their claws into. Countries that largely ignored their 'free market' thunderings, such as India and China, however, are doing rather well.

I listen to these 'free market' ideologues, and I hear medieval theologians. They are all perfectly versed in the system of thought they have swallowed. They know the hierarchies of the angels and the powers of the Seraphim and Cherubim and argue about how many angels will dance on the head of the needle.

And yet the tragedy, for us, is that none of what they know and understand corresponds with things as they really, truly are. We are led by arrogant, blind men so swaddled in the luxuries afforded to the priests of a system that they cannot think to question the catechism that rewards them.

This bloated priesthood must be humbled and overthrown. We, the people, must leave the church of the 'free market' and clear our minds.

15 Oct 08

America throws $700bn (£380bn) at their banks, we throw even more, £500bn, and still the credit markets remain frozen and the banks won't lend to companies in need. I think what's happening is that the banks are dying in the prisoner's dilemma that all first-year economics students are taught.

In the classic prisoner's dilemma, two friends are caught for a crime, but the police don't have enough evidence to convict either without a confession. Each prisoner is assured that the other prisoner will not be told what the other has said. If both confess, they each get five years. If both remain silent, they each get six months for a minor offence. But if one prisoner confesses while the other remains silent, the prisoner who confesses goes free while the other gets the full 10-year sentence.

The prisoner's dilemma points out that selfish players of the game will always choose to do what is 'best' for them in the short-term. If banks were socially minded institutions, they would lend to the wider economy because it is in all the banks' interests that the economy improves. But each bank, while it clearly sees the benefits of lending to improve the current situation, will decide that it can maximize its own profits by letting others do the socially helpful, but risky, lending, while they hoard their money and wait for better conditions.

They *all* know that lending into a failing market would help the market, but no one wants to be the one who makes loans to people in trouble. They all want to let a competitor do it. Then, when the economy improves, they can reap the reward and, at the same time, pay none of the costs. Classic prisoner's dilemma.

All the banks follow the same logic and, as a consequence, no one does the lending that might help the whole system. The result, known for the last 40 years, is that collectively they all do worse. That is why banks are not lending. The players all play beggar-thy-neighbour and so collectively lose.

And the best part of it all? Most groups of ordinary people playing prisoner's dilemma games generally cooperate as often as they cheat. The one group who consistently cheat straight away, and seem incapable of cooperating, are economists and economics students. The poetic justice would be more enjoyable if it were only the banks that were going to suffer. It's not. We all are.

19 Oct 08

Alistair Darling has responded to criticism of the bank bailout by assuring us that the banks would pay us back every penny, and more.

Come on Alistair! Credit us with a little intelligence. The economy is entering a widespread and deep recession caused in large part by the banks. They still have a stupendously large amount of debt hanging over them. As the consumer slowdown entrenches, more businesses will go to the wall creating another wave of write-downs and bailout demands. How on earth will the banks earn enough in these circumstances to pay us *and* make a profit?

Anyone can see what is going to happen. As the situation deteriorates the banks will say they cannot afford to repay on the schedule agreed. Even if in a few years they start making big profits again, they will still say they need more time if the repayments are not to force them into a repeat of the same situation. 'You'll still get paid, but tomorrow or the day after. You know we're good for it. Promise.' Previously the banks owed money to the kind of people you cannot screw around with – rich and powerful institutions. Now they have unloaded their debts on to suckers they can default upon – you and me.

But let's not be under any illusion: *we* will be paying all the time. There will be no renegotiation for *our* debt. *We* will face massive public spending cuts *and* huge tax rises. *We*, each and every taxpayer, will be paying off *their* debts with no possibility of postponement or help. *We* are going to lose our jobs, our homes and our public services to pay the debts *they* are going to default on. *They* will have their money and their bonuses, and *we* are going to be paying *them* for the pleasure.

And think of what else they have achieved. Most of the people we are bailing out are those who have long argued for massive cuts in public spending and welfare. They have not been able to achieve these goals through the ballot box, but now they will have achieved exactly what they want through economic blackmail. Bankers don't need state schools: their children go to private schools. Bankers don't need the NHS:

they go to private hospitals. Bankers don't need social services or unemployment benefits: they have bonuses and enormous pensions to cover all that. So cut it all.

There were only ever two ways out of this crisis. The clean way: force those who made the losses to take them and go bankrupt. The debts disappear because those who made bad loans just don't get paid. End of story. You then use public money to ease the pain for you and me and to restart wealth production. Don't let people tell you it couldn't be done, it could. But the wealthy get poorer, which is why it hasn't happened or even been allowed on the agenda.

The other way is to try to replace the wealth being destroyed without clearing the debts. This allows the wealthy to stay that way, but it passes their debts on to everyone else.

At the moment, we have merely taken on the debts that were about to kill the rich today, but tomorrow's debacle still awaits. Credit defaults and a more general insurance and currency trauma are just round the corner. The real economy is also contracting, and the consumer is spooked about unemployment. These things will turn the screw on the financial situation. I think the banks are now looking at the broader crisis in the real economy, and they know the chain reaction is approaching critical. The money we have given them is a tin hat in the face of a nuclear chain reaction.

It was said that in the Great Depression the market was sacrificed to save the country. Today we risk sacrificing the country to save the market.

CHAPTER 3

Fiddling at the Margins

24 Oct 08

We are now entering the second and more dangerous phase of this financial meltdown. This is when we begin to see the effects of the crisis in the real economy. Despite this, are doomsayers like me guilty of overplaying the seriousness of our situation? Is it like someone shouting 'fire' in a small building where more people get hurt in the crush than burnt by the flames?

A fair criticism if you think this is just a small fire. But what if the more appropriate analogy is being on the Titanic, the unsinkable ship?

Like the Titanic, I believe we are holed below the water. And, like the Titanic, some people are still so convinced it's unsinkable they complain about the noisy louts spoiling dinner by running about shouting that the ship is sinking. If you think the Titanic analogy is just silly, think on these few facts.

As corporations begin to go down, the credit default swaps written on their debt will blow up. When they do, those who have to pay out on the swaps lose massive amounts of money. The sheer scale of this market, which was almost totally unregulated, dwarfs absolutely everything else. It runs into tens of trillions.

Most of the institutions making these losses are highly leveraged. They never had the money to cover that many defaults because they never imagined they would have to pay out. This means even a small loss is enough to force them to have to raise more real cash to cover their losses and replace their capital holdings. This has some nasty repercussions all round.

If they sell some of their assets to raise the cash, this depresses the value of those asset types on the market making *all* the other holders of that kind of asset considerably poorer.

If they call in debts, this forces those from whom they are demanding money closer to bankruptcy. This is the situation with GMAC, the finance arm of General Motors. To stave of bankruptcy, GMAC is forcing the General Motors' dealers to whom it loaned money to pay up. Those dealers are now starting to go bust, which brings more problems for General Motors itself. Round and round and down we go.

The only other option is to go cap in hand to the government like AIG have done. So far, governments have been offering themselves as the backstop to almost every bad debt brought to them. The problem is the volume of these debts, and bets on debt, make it perfectly impossible for governments to cover all the obligations and debts. There simply isn't enough money in the world to deal with the credit default swap problem. If governments don't stop now, they will find they have their own credit rating downgraded. Once that happens to an economy like the US or the UK, things will get very nasty, very quickly.

At the moment this is still just about economics, but it soon won't be. The US has a wave of expectation that Obama is Martin Luther King and JFK combined, coming like King Arthur in the nation's time of need to save them. People are going to be very disappointed. In the next twelve weeks I think we'll find incontrovertible proof that this is going to be much worse than the 1980s and that we have everything to fear. Obama won't be able to save them.

Just a small fire? I don't think so

30 Oct 08

There comes a moment in the course of every disease when the palliative measures that had some effect at the start become irrelevant. Today's cut in US interest rate cuts are at that point.

What rate cuts are supposed to do is allow the solvent parts of the economy to get loans and try to survive the general wreck, so they are not a bad idea in theory. They are not, however, the solution to this crisis. They are simply fiddling at the margins.

Most businesses aren't looking for cheaper loans in order to expand in the current climate: they need the money because they can't make ends meet. That means, no matter how low the interest rates, no bank is going lend to them in case they default.

Or take AIG. Their deepening crisis isn't because they can't afford a bank loan: it's because they are drowning in bad credit default swap debt. It's a similar story with General Motors, Chrysler and GMAC. They aren't all going to suddenly recover if interest rates come down by another 1% because, like AIG, they are all effectively insolvent.

The problem we have is that the banks are hoarding our cash to cover their bad debts. That is why the money isn't finding its way into the rest of the economy. Unless we tackle the source of the problem, the bad debts themselves, then anything else is merely a distraction.

At the moment, we are spending all our money and credit building walls of sand in front of the incoming tide and will have none left when the inevitable happens. The evidence of failed bailouts and collapsing economies is before us. The tide of bad debt, credit default settlements and corporate bankruptcies will overwhelm our foolish sand castles. Instead of trying to hold back this tide, we would do far better to let the bankruptcies happen and use the money to help people survive the aftermath.

So go ahead, cut interest rates. It's a bit like the pilot in a crashing plane turning up the air conditioning.

Feeling comfy? Oh good.

9 Nov 08

Keep an eye on China. What they do is critical because the Chinese are the biggest buyers of US debt. They are the ones the US relies on to fund a lot of its increased borrowing.

Today the Chinese government announced a 4tn yuan (£375bn) stimulus package that sent the markets into a frenzy.

Looking at those traders, I can only see Pavlov's dogs. Someone only has to say 'stimulus package', and an automatic salivation instinct cuts in. What will this money 'stimulate'? Imports? Not likely. This is about the Chinese developing their internal market for Chinese made goods. It's about keeping a lid on growing unemployment and possible social unrest. The problem is that it has a nasty side effect for us in the West.

At precisely the moment when the US and the rest of the Western economies are going to go to the bond market to sell debt, China is starting to spend its money domestically. That points to two things. First, there will be fewer buyers for all this Western debt resulting in higher rates and possible no-bids.

Second, could it be that China will use some of its holdings of US treasuries to fund this massive stimulus package? If so, then not only will the Chinese not be buying new bonds, but they may also be dumping previously issued ones onto the market. If you are sitting in the US or UK treasury anxiously needing to find buyers for all your new debt then this doesn't bode well.

10 Nov 08

Rumours abound that Alistair Darling will be announcing tax cuts in the forthcoming pre-budget report. Poor old Alistair has tried getting money into the economy through the banks, and largely failed, so now he thinks he will try us idiots in the street. The only problem is I don't think consumers will oblige either.

What the high street and factories want is for consumers to buy stuff, but what the consumer now wants is to pay off the mortgage and the credit card debt. This, of course, will simply return the money to the banks who will simply sit on it to cover their bad debts. That's why tax cuts won't save us either.

Fiscal stimulus helps people who need just a bit more money to pay the mortgage and buy what they need. What it won't do, in the current situation, is rescue the economy and restart another consumer orgy. When people are so far underwater with debt that extra money just gets sucked away.

We can't consume our way out of this mess, nor should we. Look at what happened to us in the boom times. We bought new cars every few years, perpetually made over our houses, took cheap flights to all corners of the globe and paid for it, not because we were earning so much more, but on credit because our property had gone up in value.

What we created was debt, not wealth. And debt is to real wealth as a shadow is to the object casting it. It's much easier to inflate the shadow. The only problem is shadows, while impressively large while the sun shines, disappear when the rain comes. And that is exactly what happened.

Now our house price bubble has burst everyone is suddenly, and rightly, afraid of their debt and anxious to reduce it as much as possible. That's why spending won't return to boom time levels of consumption anytime soon.

The good times are over. Debt fuelled consumer capitalism has been knocked out cold and neither Maynard Keynes nor Milton Freidman can revive it.

24 Nov 08

Yet more losses and more bailouts. It was just announced that Citigroup has had to be bailed out to the tune of $20bn. The US government have also agreed to guarantee over $300bn in dodgy loans and toxic assets on the bank's books.

Why continue with this insanity? We are just digging ourselves deeper and deeper into a debt from which we may never recover. And there are many more bank losses to come. Most of the debt-backed assets held on the banks' books have still not been downgraded by the rating agencies. They will be.

Every time there is a mortgage default, a loan default or a company bankruptcy, more downwards pressure is put on the value of those assets. More downgrades mean more losses. As the bank becomes worth less, it has less capital to support its remaining liabilities. At some point, when the capital requirement becomes too low, they must raise more capital or face a bank run. This is why we will soon see a lengthening queue of City suits with signs asking for the nation to 'spare £50bn for a poor banker.'

So far, our politicians have been only too willing to give. Yet in their obsession to help their banking friends they have closed their eyes to one fundamental fact: we cannot simply go on and on getting deeper and deeper into debt. The debt market is not bottomless. Someone has to buy that debt. The question as to whether they will or not is going to dominate our lives for the coming years.

Just look at what is happening in the US. To fund the bailouts the government is about to start issuing monumental amounts of its own debt. But now, as we have seen, it doesn't look like the Chinese are going to go on buying forever. If they reduce their buying, or even start selling, that is going to spell big problems for the US. How are they going to fund their debt levels then?

And then there is the unintended consequence of US debt issuance. In these terribly turbulent times investors want a safe haven, and US national debt is still seen as the last place likely to default. But such are the amounts of debt the US government needs to sell that everyone else is being squeezed out of the market. The demand for corporate debt is drying up. This means the American government's insatiable appetite for debt is helping kill off the very companies it hopes will create jobs and growth in the US economy.

There is also the effect on other countries. To compete with US debt, other weaker nations, like the UK, will find they have to pay higher interest. This will increase investors' doubts about our ability to pay back what we are borrowing. As those doubts grow, they will only lend us money over shorter and shorter terms. We will have to keep returning to the markets at ever shorter intervals. This means, as our debt payments become due, the schedule of tax rises and public service cuts will be largely dictated by those to whom we owe money.

That is what we are letting ourselves in for.

25 Nov 08

All the money so far still hasn't been enough. The Fed has just announced they are to spend an EXTRA $800bn buying up more bad debts from the banks.

There was a time when medical orthodoxy said that applying leeches to bleed the patient was the cure for all ills. Madness – apply leaches. Gout – apply leeches. Cancer – apply leaches. They were so wedded to one theory that they couldn't think of anything else. It didn't matter how many people failed to respond to the treatment. They still never changed what they did. We are in exactly that position now with the economy.

I have this distressing feeling that the policy advisors and officials are so utterly unable to withdraw from the liquidity model that they continue to pull levers which are no longer attached to anything. So when they pull and nothing happens, they just pull harder.

Every bailout fails, but instead of dealing with the fundamental and systemic problem of the underlying bad debt they continue with more of the same 'bail the banks and beg the consumer to spend' policies that have failed so spectacularly. We are being impoverished and shackled to an unimaginably large debt by leaders and experts who cannot imagine anything else.

Each one of their rescues not only hasn't done what they assured us it would do, but has not even prevented events from getting worse.

At what point, after how many failures, do people begin to wonder if the paradigm being followed might just not accord with reality? Their theory said it was lack of liquidity. They injected vast liquidity, but the problems got worse not better. They rescued insolvent institutions to restore confidence, but confidence evaporated and all stock markets fell off a cliff.

All the currently proposed solutions are doomed to fail for one simple reason: they are not attempting to revive the real economy directly. They are all designed to revive the machinery of debt in the belief that this is the way to help the economy. It isn't.

The problem is that the banks' various mortgage-backed assets were never designed to turn a profit simply by the underlying loan being paid back. They were designed to pay off by the 'value' of the underlying asset itself increasing. This means, for the mountain of debt-backed assets to make their owners super rich again, we must return to a speculation-fuelled, bubble economy. Leveraged debt requires leveraged growth to pay it off.

In their blind panic, I fear what our leaders are hoping to do is reanimate the bloated corpse of debt-backed finance to see it emerging like the proverbial alien from the body of the 'emergency recovery plan'.

Do we want them to re-animate the monster that got us into this mess in the first place? I don't want policies that try to reignite another consumer binge and reinflate another housing bubble. Most of all, I don't want the banks to be able to create, trade and speculate on the ups and downs of debt-backed derivatives. This kind of speculative, removed from the real world capitalism has enriched a tiny number and promised to enrich the rest of us by trickle-down. It has, in fact, impoverished us instead.

30 Nov 08

If throwing billions at the banks' bad debts wasn't enough, there is now serious talk that several of the worst banks should be nationalised. This is madness piled upon insanity.

Could people please think carefully about the word *nationalisation*. It is in danger of becoming a magic word. If we nationalise the banks, do we really want to take on and nationalise all their debts and undisclosed obligations? If we do then the debt will grow well beyond £1.5 trillion.

Nationalising is, in my opinion, a terrible option. Of course, handing public money over to private banks is an outrage, but does that somehow make buying a potentially bottomless liability a better idea? Both are desperately stupid.

If you nationalise the banks, you make the taxpayer liable for the titanic amount of undisclosed debts. Despite all the banks' protestations to the contrary, the debt is still there, salted away in level three assets and offshore, off-balance sheet vehicles. It hasn't gone away.

That's why if we nationalise the banks, we are nationalising a debt that has the potential power to bankrupt the country. In fact, that is what our stupid leaders are allowing to happen now, in slow motion, via one asinine bailout after another. These still undisclosed debts are a dirty bomb just waiting to go off. Let it blow up the banks, not us.

3 Dec 08

Yet another 'expert' on the radio this morning saying there is no alternative to bailing out the banks. One of his reasons is that if the banks go, so do our pensions.

Of course our pensions are tied to the fortunes and demise of the banks. Their financial experts made sure of that. But our pensions are also tied up in lots of other stuff. Manufacturing, and farming. Making stuff. Not just speculating on it.

If we carry on with the bailouts, every last bit of your pension will be poisoned. It will all go bad. Just watch what is going to happen next year and weep; no bailout is going to stop it.

That's why we need to purge the bad debts rather than keep letting them poison the economy and our pensions. If we clear the debts, your pension will nose-dive and then start to recover. Instead of pouring money uselessly into bailing out the banks we could use it to ameliorate the short-term, shortfalls in pensions. They would then be based on a real currency having real value and be invested in solvent enterprises.

I am not advocating the pain of clearing the debts because I think it will be a great afternoon out for all the family. It will be quite dreadful. I advocate it because it is both necessary for any lasting and equitable recovery to take place at all and because it is going to happen no matter what we want or what our politicians and assembled experts say.

We need to accept the short-term pain of many of the big banks going down for our long-term gain. At the moment, we are facing long-term pain for vast swathes of the population to pay for the short-term gain of the banks.

5 Dec 08

Now the knife begins to turn. In the US, the news of 533,000 newly unemployed in a SINGLE MONTH was just announced. That is much worse than 'the plan' calls for. All we need now is to order lots of flat caps, a bumper load of black and white film to record it on, and we're there:

Great Depression 2.0. Make no mistake; this storm is only just getting warmed up. The US is a tinderbox just waiting for a spark. People there, ordinary people with a flag outside their house, are angry in way I have never seen in twenty years of going to the US.

On a very recent visit, I met a woman who worked in the Cleveland school district. She said their fastest growing problem was kids who could not do their homework, were not very clean and were not getting a good evening meal because at night they and their families were sleeping in cars in car parks. In the winter, Cleveland gets to minus 20 Fahrenheit. How do you think that is going to work?

At least here we have a welfare state and the National Health Service. In the States there is no social welfare net to speak of. The poor have zip. I met a family recently whose father died because he couldn't afford the medicines for his heart condition. No insurance, no health service, just an untimely death and a family wondering what they were going to do. That is the reality of the Land of the Free for many, many poor people.

That is why I think there will be blood this winter in at least one American city. Politicians everywhere seem to have forgotten that hunger and cold are all you need. There are lots of homeless families living in their cars this summer. When it's well below zero and your family is living in a car, I don't think the situation ends peacefully.

2008 was a breeze compared to what is going to happen in 2009.

CHAPTER 4

Wake Up People!

9 Dec 08

In Greece the rioting is still continuing after the police shot dead a teenage boy at the weekend. I wonder if this rioting is really just about the police shooting someone or if it is about something more.

Because of the economic situation in Greece, 'experts' have already been talking about the need for severe cuts in social spending. I think that threat plus Greece's general economic woes are at the root of why one such incident can spark such a violent response. And it's not just Greece where people are protesting. In the US, one group of workers at Republic Windows Corp has already begun an illegal occupation of their workplace. They are protesting about the company being forced into bankruptcy by Bank of America refusing to extend a loan. I think we are going to be seeing a lot more of this both in Europe and the US.

It will all be called anarchism or mindless violence, and I have no doubt some of it will be, but much of it will be people's frustration at finding out that they, and not the bankers, are the ones who are being made to pay for the crisis.

Our governments will make ordinary people pay because the politicians don't have the courage or understanding to really tackle the underlying problems. What all our governments will be quite ready to do, though, is bring out the police to deal with any public dissent and unrest.

They will do that because our creditors, the people we are begging to buy our governments' gilts and treasuries, will demand that they do. No one will buy our debt and fund all this spending if they think, for an instant, that social unrest could endanger us paying them what we owe.

Our governments will, like the First World War generals, throw us all into the meat grinder before they will think they might be wrong. But they are wrong.

12 Dec 08

Here we go. The FTSE, the Dow Jones, Hong Kong's Hang Seng, Japan's Nikkei… stock markets all over the world fell dramatically this morning as people got news that the bailout package aimed at saving the US car industry had collapsed.

Either a last minute deal is done whereby some of the money from the Troubled Asset Relief Program (TARP) is used to help the car industry – which Bush and Paulson don't want – or some of the big companies go into Chapter 11 bankruptcy protection.

If they do go bankrupt, that's going to mean thousands of workers turfed out onto the streets and thrown into poverty and destitution. But it is also going to cause an earthquake in the credit default market. So much paper was written on General Motors' bonds that if they go down, the fear is they could take a lot of big finance players with them.

And then there's the news that top commercial real estate company General Growth Properties (GGP) will probably file for bankruptcy this evening. Why is this significant? Well, it's a good, clear sign for everyone that the property collapse has now spread to the larger commercial market. That's going to be about as welcome as an outbreak of dysentery on a long-haul flight.

Commercial property is like a very large version of the buy-to-let market, and it's now starting to default

Most of those who own skyscrapers, shopping malls and other commercial spaces took out enormous loans to cover their costs. With property prices across the sectors plummeting, they now owe a lot, lot more than the building is actually worth. It is negative equity with gargantuan nobs on. This is making the bankers who lent them the money very nervous. The banks are refusing to roll over loans and are calling in payments. Because many mall owners can't meet the payments whole shopping malls are already being foreclosed, which is putting even viable retailers out of business. And we all know how it goes from there.

All this, of course, while the banks are posting yet more losses and promising more job cuts.

Anyone who believes that the wheezing liars in government and the market fraudsters still know what to do just need to look at events.

13 Dec 08
Pressure is beginning to mount on sterling. So much so that Gordon Brown felt moved to declare in the Sun yesterday that he would *not* be scrapping the pound – at least not for the foreseeable future. This was in response to calls by the president of the European Commission, José Manuel Barroso, for Britain to join the single currency.

The reality is that the UK may be forced to join the euro no matter what Brown says. Our entire 'recovery plan' is predicated on the international debt market agreeing to buy our gilts, but there is already too much debt flooding the market and much, much more to come.

If the debt buyers have worries that the pound will continue to decline then they will not want to buy debt denominated in pounds. They will insist that we issue our debt in a currency they think they can trust: the euro. If they do make this demand, Britain will have to join the euro. You simply can't issue debt in a currency other than your own. It is economic suicide. South American countries have done it … which rather makes my point.

Some people here will get in a terrible 'little Englander' flap about it and run around with their eyes bulging out screaming about the loss of sovereignty, but it doesn't matter a jot what they, or Brown, think. In the end, it won't be a political choice: the international bond market will make that choice for us. Brown knows this.

15 Dec 08
The pound hit another new low against the euro this morning. Why is it that currency speculators are buying other currencies rather than pounds? I think the answer is that they have fundamental worries about Britain. They think the pound has further to fall, so no one wants to hold too much of the stuff.

Take one interesting fact: the price of credit default swaps on UK sovereign debt is now higher than for McDonalds! That means the debt markets – the people from whom we are trying to raise money for all our bailouts and stimulus packages – think there is more chance that the UK will default than McDonalds.

Part of their worry is whether any future government will have the will to enforce the cuts necessary to make the repayments on the debt. The cuts will have to be huge, and they know it. It's just that no one wants to say it at the moment. Public service pensions are going to be first in line. You only have to see the recent report by the Confederation of British Industry (CBI), the self-declared 'Voice of Business', to see the forces lining up wanting to make a bonfire of public service pensions. The problem for the debt market is that they aren't sure the government will be able to keep a lid on the unrest when they try and push through such cuts.

16 Dec 08

The governor of the Bank of England, Mervyn King, wrote to Chancellor Alistair Darling today saying that 'additional measures' to support the banking system would probably be needed if we are to avoid the danger of deflation later next year.

The point, which Mr King seems to miss, is that there is nothing of any consequence the government, or the Bank of England, can do about deflation. The deflationary forces are simply too massive. Just take a look at the next wave approaching the beach.

In 2009, it is estimated that British banks alone will declare a further £70bn in write-downs. Why will this happen? Because they are all holding securities or derivatives based on American Alt-A, Option ARM, and commercial mortgages, which are all approaching crisis. When this new wave of mortgage defaults breaks, it will create another, deeper round of the credit crunch.

Option ARMs are mortgages where, for an introductory period, you can choose how much to pay or not pay – all the way down to paying nothing. The interest you don't pay gets added on to your mortgage. You can keep adding until your loan grows to 125% of the original amount. Then, at the end of the introductory period, this new colossal amount – the original mortgage *plus* the interest owed – *all* gets put on to a much higher rate. The market, unsurprisingly, expects massive default rates to really get going in May-June.

The market also expects huge defaults with Alt-A mortgages. Nearly four million small businesses in the US have this type of mortgage, and 1.2 million are already 60 days overdue with their payments.

As these very large sets of mortgages default, all the mortgage-backed securities written on them will, at some stage, have to be devalued. The problem for the banks is that because they are so insanely leveraged even very small losses can wipe out a lot of their capital. That's the joy of leverage: builds you up and then hurts like hell when it knocks you down.

As these securities lose value, the banks will, by law, have to raise new cash in order to plug the gaping hole in their balance sheets. The problem for the banks is that they don't have the money. Their shareholders are tapped out, and the sovereign funds will tell them to sod off. Guess who they'll come to then? You and me, yet again! And the governments will make stern noises, look concerned, and then say, 'Of course sir, how much would you like sir.'

We got into this mess by sitting and listening to the fatuous and self-serving assurances of the financial experts. Now we are sitting around letting the self-same economic experts tell us how to get out of it. They were greedy, amoral, short-sighted, totally self-serving then; what makes anyone think they are different now? WAKE UP PEOPLE!

Economic decisions should not be above democracy! They are not technical questions that we must leave to the 'experts', especially those who created the chaos. When illegal wars were started, when coalmines were closed, when nuclear weapons were stationed, people felt moved to protest in the streets. We need to start an organization like Stop the War but dedicated to stopping the bank bailouts.

To get a feel for how much worse it's going to get in 2009 look at the line being formed for US government bailouts alone. And it's not just the banks. Don't listen to the politicians look at the numbers.

Carmakers – bailed.

GMAC – the lending arm of General Motors – bailed.

Steelmakers – requested a bailout this week.

Life Insurers – bailout being considered.

And then there is California, the fifth largest economy in the world. It will officially run out of money in 60-90 days. The Great State will be bankrupt and is already planning to issue tax rebates not in cash but in IOUs. That is how far we have come already.

WE NEED TO GET OUT ONTO THE STREETS!

One thing we can do to protest immediately is to move our bank accounts from one of the failing banks to one of those which did not get into trouble – the Cooperative bank and any number of smaller building societies in the UK, some regional banks in the US. If we do it soon, we have a chance to stop further vast debt enslavement from more doomed-to-fail bailouts.

Simply moving our accounts and those of any organization we belong to – schools, councils, clubs and unions – would help force an end to the ruination of the country, the forcible enslavement of a generation and the trumping of democratic control by economic fear.

It is easy to do; it costs nothing. Our money will be just as safe, probably safer. We will get the same (laughable) interest. All our direct debits and standing orders will still work; our money will be protected and, most importantly, we will have given the bankers the only message they care about. The media would sure as hell pick up on it, and once they did the banks and the government would panic.

If the bailed out banks have all the valuable assets they claim to have then there should be no problem with people moving their money. If it's the case that these assets are virtually worthless, then it's not a good idea to put your money in an insolvent bank.

Your money in an insolvent bank is dead money. It is not being lent out to businesses that could use it to create employment. It is being hoarded. Move your money to a clean bank or building society and that institution can lend it.

It would only take a few per cent of deposit accounts to be moved from the bailed out banks into the few sound banks and building societies, and we could force what the government will not: the collapse of the insolvent banks.

Moving accounts would tip the losing bank towards the brink, and when it did the government would want to step in again with your money. The only way it's going to stop is if they get a clear message that we won't stand for it. If a significant number of people did this, it would force the financial world to their knees and the politicians to change course.

It's a simple idea for ordinary people to take decisive action to forcefully, but legally, put a stop to an utterly doomed policy of bail and bust. Those who made the bad investments and loans would be wiped out. That's life. The rest of us, the vast majority, could then live on without being made to pay off their debts.

Vote with your money, and they'll listen. If no more than 5% of depositor accounts moved, that bank would implode. The power is yours. USE IT.

2 Jan 09

The start of the new year and we get predictions of an even worse year ahead for house prices as the number of new mortgages fall to a record low. But this isn't about house prices any more. They're just the barometer. If house price falls and negative equity were our only problem, we'd be laughing. We have to move on!

We have spent well over a trillion dollars and our governments have grand plans to spend much more. But all that spending is money borrowed or printed, and in the end it all amounts to the same thing: debt.

What happens when we have to start paying it back? Paying the bankers debts will cripple welfare, NHS, education and local government. There won't be any area of public service spending that isn't brutally butchered. Even if our nation should slide into a depression, the owners of the IOUs will regard them as binding. The rich may not take our poverty very seriously, but they take their own very damn seriously. They will expect whatever tax hikes and welfare cuts are required to make sure we do pay them back.

As for those who are still thinking this is just another boom and bust cycle, or even another recession like previous ones, I have to say I think you are terribly wrong. I don't think you'll even see 1% growth for a while. Contraction, unemployment and social service cutbacks are what you are going to get. And the bond market agrees. If you look at the spreads on US bonds, the market is pricing in a massive and sustained amount of deflation. They really are pricing in something closer to a depression rather than a simple recession.

That is the grim future we are all facing, and yet the whole debate about what we should be doing has been sucked down an intellectual sink hole where it is just tumbling over and over in the dark. The entire discussion is framed within the unquestioned parameters of the need to bail out the banks and provide stimulus actions to boost the economy. No alternatives are ever discussed.

In many ways, much economic journalism, in this country at least, seems to be 'embedded' the way journalists were with the military in Iraq. They are so totally dependent on the good will of the City to give them access to titbits of inside information that they can't imagine actually questioning the hegemonic assumptions upon which the financial world is based. It has meant there has been a dearth of open discussion of the assumptions that have captured all policy decisions.

It's like listening to First World War generals discussing the latest battle plan. No matter how completely the strategy failed the last time, no matter what carnage resulted, they learn nothing and do the same again and again – only bigger each time.

Nowhere in this debate is it ever allowed to suggest that the real problem is the need to clear the system of the millstone of bad debts. We're just not allowed to hear that the least painful and fastest solution is to force the bad debts into the open and replace the old, bankrupt banks with new banks.

The fact is we would survive without the bad banks and their bad debts. What we will most definitely *not* survive is trying to take all their bad debts into the Bank of England. That will most definitely lead to a crisis of biblical proportions.

In the end, I think we will have to repudiate the debt payments, but does anyone really think the government – of whatever party – and the economic interests they represent will allow it? Imagine the flight of gilt buyers away from the pound if they thought there was any chance at all of repudiation. Just to get spoken about seriously in public could be enough to cause a fatal flight from our debt.

Would even talk of such a possibility then be considered a threat to national security? Would organising support for such an opinion be allowed? And if no party runs on a repudiate the debt platform what recourse will you have? Protest? Mass civil disobedience?

This is far more serious than a bit of negative equity and a house price collapse. Don't sit like children while the grown-ups act. Decisions are being made that are more disastrous and far-reaching than the Poll Tax, mine closures or even the war in Iraq.

We must protest now before it's too late.

CHAPTER 5

A Suicide Note

12 Jan 09

This is when things start getting very dangerous and very desperate. Banks won't lend, consumers won't consume, and governments have fewer and fewer people they can tax. What do they do then? Answer: print. And if they are a bit nervous about it, like the British government, they can call it something else, like 'quantitative easing' (QE), and pass a law to obscure how much money is printed and when.

Legislation is now going through parliament to reverse a law put in place over 160 years ago. This law said the Bank of England had to make public how much money it was printing. The new law will allow the bank to delay publishing details. It will make the Bank of England one of the most, if not *the* most secretive central bank in the industrial world.

Bear in mind, printing isn't a 'policy option': it's done out of utter panic and desperation when countries consider they have no other choice. I believe worries about not being able to raise money through debt issuance are part of the reason they are now contemplating taking such a drastic step. And Britain isn't alone.

Spain's sovereign debt was downgraded the other day from AAA, making it more costly for them sell their debt. Germany had lots of bonds remaining unsold after its last auction, and the US is in trouble because both Japan and China look like they want to buy a lot less US debt.

In a normal situation, resorting to printing would produce price inflation as more money chases the same number of goods. Because our situation is far from normal the central banks are keeping their fingers crossed that it won't have this effect. They hope they are just replacing money that is bleeding away. In this case, the money seeping away is the banks' debt-backed paper that has lost most of its value. The new money being pumped in is to replace that lost value. The thinking is that we're not really inflating the money supply because we're only replacing what is being destroyed.

If we print modestly, we may well get away with not causing hyperinflation or a currency crash. But a modest amount will not solve the problem of replacing all the worthless paper securities held by the banks. The collapse in value of these securities and derivatives still has a long way to go. Did you know mortgage defaults in California increased by 100% in December? And those mortgages were securitised and sold on.

That's why there are still massive losses to come. If governments do try to replace all the banks' rubbish with new dollars, euros and pounds then we run the very real risk of people wondering what real value stands behind so much newly printed money.

As soon as they wonder seriously about that, you get a currency crash and hyperinflation. This is the very real risk of printing, but it looks like that's where we're headed. They are only saying it is OK to print because nothing else is working. Not because it's a good or wise idea.

16 Jan 09

As the central bankers get ready to gear up the printing presses the banking losses continue. Citigroup was given a massive bailout a few weeks ago, now it's Bank of America's turn. Today it was given $20bn by the US government and a guarantee of $118bn on likely future losses.

This isn't a policy! It's a bad poker player gambling everything he has, and more. He has a useless hand but has tried to stay in the game. He has raised on nothing and been raised again. The idiot then tries to bluff and throws his house into the pot after all his cash has already gone. This is the 'policy' the bankers are encouraging.

And the sad thing for the government? They are not going to win. Shares in both banks nose-dived 18% yesterday. Bank shares are not recovering and won't. The shareholders are selling because they know they are going to lose more if they hold out. They worry that more injections of cash will dilute or wipe out their shares. Even the bondholders may get shafted.

To try and save the situation some people have suggested the creation of a 'bad bank' into which all the toxic assets could be dumped. This has been mooted for months, but the banks have been playing chicken with the governments for one simple reason: it all boils down to what we, the taxpayer, are going to fork out for the so-called assets. (Remember these are assets the banks cannot sell and have absolutely no prospect of selling at anytime in the foreseeable future.)

If we create a bad bank to take their assets, and we pay close to what the banks say they should be worth, then the taxpayer will be robbed of billions. If we pay the banks what they are actually worth, then the banks would go bankrupt the next day. So it's hardly a surprise that they haven't gone for this solution. They are waiting until we are so scared that we'll pay whatever they say. The bad bank idea is a crook's charter.

The banks are dead. Look around. Is this system working? Are the banks doing their job? No! Who is being served by saving these rotten banks? Not you and me.

It's as if several large ships proudly carrying the British flag were suddenly holed below the water line. In such an event, there would be immediate reaction and a determination to save all those aboard. But what would happen if, on inspection, we found each ship was carrying huge cargoes of sweating dynamite – the naval equivalent of the banks' deteriorating loans and toxic assets?

At this point, I would abandon ship and be thankful she went to the bottom with her explosive cargo. But no! The owners of the ship, and those whose cargo she is carrying, want to save their fortunes. So, despite being fatally holed and carrying a chemically unstable cargo, we invest more and more money and effort in increasingly vain attempts to save her. What we should do, of course, is let the boat and her cargo sink to the bottom and use our money to build a smaller, lighter and safer ship to do the job better. We should do the same with the banks.

We need to clear the debt by marking it to market in an orderly fashion, but we need to do it forcefully – no cheating and hiding. There are quite a few commentators, not just me, who are proposing this. It's not rocket science.

We should set dates and deadlines for the banks by which time *all* the banks' assets and holdings, in every form, have to be either marked-to-market, actually sold, or a buyer found and a bid made. More than one date should be set so the process can be phased. Anything which has not been marked, sold or settled by the time given would be seized, valued and marked-to-market by force. No excuses would be allowed about impaired markets and the rest. Depositors' money would be guaranteed up to the set limit.

Firm deadlines would give everyone the same chance and provide a level and fair playing field. It also gives people time. It will force the market to work and the losses to be realised.

Before this process is underway, we should take the money currently being wasted on futile bailouts and capitalise brand new clean banks that have no bad debts. With such banks in place the banking system would not collapse. What would collapse would be the network of currently existing walking-dead banks. They and their debts would expire.

In the UK we could use the Post Office as the basis for one good bank. There are plenty of solvent banks in the US that could be used over there. We could offer shares in the new banks to investors. Everyone would know the new banks would be solvent with no bad debts or unknown obligations. Investors would be queuing up to invest since these would be profitable and safe havens. Even other banks would lend to them.

The 'good bank' would do what any bank should and can do. It would give businesses a lender who would lend. It would provide a place to put your money that isn't at risk of imploding under the weight of undeclared debts. The 'good bank' would also have the confidence of other financial institutions. In short, we would have a banking system that works and is solvent. Something we don't have at the moment.

This plan does not wave a magic wand and make all the losses go away. Nothing can do that. But having good, clean working banks puts a firm foundation in place on which to build a recovery. Instead, what we are doing now is trying to build a recovery on top of a swamp of rotting debt.

Their solution is simply about maintaining the power structure that benefits them. But it does so by means of *our* enslavement to pay off *their* debts. The good bank solution is the only solution that puts the welfare of the vast majority of people before the desire of the wealthy to remain wealthy.

With good, new, solvent banks in place there *are* things we can do to lessen the chances of this madness happening again. We need to look at the problems and deal with those. The problems in my opinion are leverage, and the unregulated creation of the debt-backed currency whose collapse is the cause of this crisis.

We can prevent leverage by setting strict limits. This was done after the Great Depression. Those limits were revoked in the last decade by the very bankers who are now in charge. That greedy stupidity is a large part of our present misery.

The laws regulating the rating agencies must be changed so the agencies are clearly independent from those whom they are supposed to be regulating. which is not the case at the moment.

Debt insurance must be revolutionised. The monoline insurers, those who insure the bond market, are a fiction and should be put to the sword. They are the walking dead anyway. Credit default swaps need to be brought under a clearing house where capital reserves and collateral are carefully scrutinised.

Next, we should put a tax on financial transactions. It needs to be small enough that it doesn't harm ordinary people, but big enough to make high volume, high-risk speculation less profitable. We should separate retail from investment banking.

These are modest and practical proposals. I am not the only one advocating them. They would work. They would bankrupt many of the wealthy players but protect the vast bulk of taxpayers. The pain would be short-tem and directed at those who deserved it. Under their plan the pain is long-term and directed at the majority of the population who don't deserve it.

19 Jan 09

Their insanity continues apace. Alistair Darling announced yet another massive bailout to the banks this morning, reassuring us that we would all be much worse without it. A central part of the new bailout is a plan for the government to insure the banks against future losses on their toxic assets.

This could really be the most expensive suicide note in history! This plan is exchanging a possible run on the banks with a possible run on the whole country, its tax base and its currency.

Let's be clear about what we are insuring. We are going to insure securities and derivatives based on mortgage and corporate debts – pieces of paper that the insurance world now refuses to insure. Insurers such as AIG, who did insure this stuff, are now bankrupt. Bailed out three times already for over $100bn and still dropping like a stone. What, therefore, makes anyone think the UK government should get into exactly the same business? If there were any chance that this insurance would turn a profit then commercial insurers would be fighting over it. They are not; we shouldn't be either.

The central question for us is to what level we are going to insure these assets. If it's up to near the full face value, which is what will please the markets, then as a nation this is a suicide note signed on behalf of us all by the chancellor.

Why are they doing this? The reasoning is that the banks are going to continue to take massive losses. They all know this, but governments don't want to have to pay huge lumps of cash to cover these losses before they have to. The advantage with insurance is that it is only paid as and when each asset has to come to the market to be formally declared dead. This means governments don't have to make one vast lump sum payment. Paying the banks this way also has one big political advantage for the government. Bailouts are public and large. Insurance, on the other hand, means the real costs to the public can be dribbled away in private with no public announcement.

As for those who say the banks will pay us a premium. Well, that premium will be paid with the cash we gave them six months ago.

The big problem for us is that our own losses are potentially unlimited. Darling says they will declare a limit, but the plan will only 'restore confidence' if it is seen to work over the long-term. This means if the banks reach the set limit, the government will be forced to extend it. They will tell us we can't 'waste all the money spent so far' and that we 'must see it through.' That's the logic of the bailouts. That's why underwriting these losses is insanity. It's a potentially bottomless pit.

And remember, we don't even have the money we are pledging now, let alone for what is to come. We have to borrow it, and pretty soon we won't be able to do that. The bond market is glutted with offerings of sovereign debt already. And it won't just be us having problems. Even the Americans are going to find things get a little hairy, especially if the Chinese get the jitters about buying US debt.

Our leaders' plan isn't working and won't work. We are simply exchanging a financial crisis for a much worse political one in the not too distant future. The debts will eventually cause a big financial institution or an entire country to fail and start a chain reaction larger than the last.

Will this happen next week, or the week after? No. It won't happen before even more extreme bailout measures are forced on us. Like losing gamblers they will want to keep having one last throw of the dice.

27 Jan 09

As the crisis deepens people are looking around for scapegoats, and some are laying the blame purely with the politicians who failed to regulate the banks.

I agree the politicians are criminally at fault, but to blame all our troubles on a lack of regulation is like a murderer blaming loose gun laws for his deciding to murder someone. Agreed, loose gun laws are an idiot's charter, but it takes an idiot to pull the trigger. Those idiots were men in sharp suits and big braces.

Let's remind ourselves of exactly what happened should anyone be in doubt. The global banking industry, not happy being limited to the flows of nationally regulated money, sliced and diced mortgages and loans turning them into a new currency of debt-backed securities and derivatives. This became their own private and utterly unregulated currency beyond the control of any nation state. *They* did this, not the politicians.

The problem was, and is, that the banks debased their new currency as fast as they could. Prices were inflated and mortgages were sold knowing that the borrower had zero chance of ever replaying the loan.

Let's take self-certified mortgages. Here a blind eye was turned to the real ability of the person to pay back the loan.

Instead bankers counted on property price inflation to take care of it all. On that belief, you could sell a house to a corpse. Ninja loans (No Income, No Job, No Assets) were the result. And why not, if everyone up the chain got a fat bonus on volume of trade with no regard to viability?

And then there is the 'insurance'. When they traded insurance on their investments they knew that not one of the insuring firms, or credit default swap sellers, had sufficient capital to make good on their promises. They knew. Everyone knew. Hell, even I knew. Firms I could name had over $3billion 'insured' with only $80million in capital!

That wasn't an accident. Many leading bankers lobbied Congress hard for the relaxing of the rules restricting leverage. The rules were relaxed, and that has been a major factor in this crisis. They didn't break any law because they rewrote the laws so they didn't have to. But they should be blamed.

They didn't think it mattered because they didn't think anyone would ever have to pay. The whole deal depended on a bubble market to inflate the value of the property. They all knew everything was reliant on this bubble continuing to get bigger and bigger and go higher and higher. Some were so stupid they actually really believed it 'could only go up.' So when the bubble did burst they were the ones left holding all the worthless paper they had created.

In such circumstances what do you do then?

Well if you are an unscrupulous, amoral apology for a human being, someone solely driven by greed and motivated by money, the answer is simple: you tell the craven politicos and hired hacks that 'the world will end' if any of you are allowed to go bust. You get the politicians to force the people, at whatever cost, to pay *your* debts. You lie, tell any lie at all, to make sure they bail you out. Nothing can come between you and your wealth.

And it was so. And here we are with City apologists puffing themselves out in righteous defence of the people who raped us.

The financial world engaged in a decade of knowingly reckless actions undertaken for personal greed that are now hurting our children. If a man punched your child in the face would you remain composed and not talk of blame? Or would you want to make sure that person was never allowed near children again.

Let me make myself clear. I am not scapegoating. I am not blaming the bankers and assorted financial experts for something that someone else did. I am blaming *them* for what *they* did.

Aaah. That feels better.

3 Feb 09

We must remember to keep a watch on China. News of the downturn in their economy, with 26 million now out of work, doesn't bode well. The more problems the Chinese have at home, the less US and UK debt they will buy. And that is a serious problem. They have already cut back their buying of US debt but are still the largest holders. That might change if the US starts printing in earnest.

If that happens, the Chinese are going to see the value of the US bonds they hold inflated away. There is no way China will let this happen. I think, in that situation, they would call the US Treasury and say quietly, politely and reasonably that if the US tries to shaft them through inflation, they will have no choice but to sell their holdings, all of them, at discount prices.

Selling those holdings at a time when the US is trying to issue $2 trillion in new debt over the next year or two would be catastrophic. This discounted debt would flood the market and make new debt impossible to sell. The US would be screwed. It is the financial world's version of Mutual Assured Destruction. And it's not just a theory.

When the crisis broke, the Chinese held nearly $400bn of Fannie and Freddie paper, but those holdings didn't carry the explicit guarantee of the US government. This would have left the Chinese with a vault full of empty promises, feeling mightily aggrieved. Rumour has it that there were a number of calls from China to Henry Paulson at the US Treasury with Chinese officials threatening to dump ALL their holdings of US debt if Paulson wouldn't guarantee the Fannie and Freddie paper. True or not, the US Treasury quickly stepped in to backstop the debt.

So watch what happens. Every report of contraction in Chinese growth and their government spending domestically is cutting off the supply of cash, without which Obama and Brown's plans just don't work. It's a simple point.

18 Feb 09

There seems to be early evidence of capital flight *out* of the US. If it is confirmed, it would be news indeed.

I think the critical point will come when the bailouts get so large, and there is so much bad news, that the buyers of US debt start to back off. I don't think we're near that yet, although there has been a slowdown in both Chinese and Japanese buying. And, of course, as for corporate paper, forget it. It is already the case that foreign buyers of Freddie and Fannie debt have dried up totally. Now the only corporate paper moving is stuff explicitly backed by the US government, but even they cannot backstop everything. It would double US debt over night. It's the same problem we're having in Britain, only much bigger. These are the tremors that hint at an earthquake, but so far no one has ever predicted an earthquake from counting the tremors.

Last year I said there would be riots in an American city this winter. I think I will be proved wrong on that. I think there will be unrest, but not so soon. There is still an aura of hope surrounding Obama, but quite how long that will last I am not sure.

Here, it will be interesting to see if there is a coalition of unrest around the G20. If there is, I think we could begin to enter a phase where civil unrest and protest begin to have an impact on economics. Once the reality of having to pay for the bailouts hits home in tangible cuts to services, at just the time people are losing their jobs, well... all bets are off.

19 Feb 09
Read this and weep: 'The government's rescue of some of Britain's biggest banks could push the country's debt levels up to 150% of national income, from a three-decade high of 48% now. The liabilities of Lloyds and RBS, if taken on the public purse could *add* (my italics) between £1tn and £1.5tn to public sector debt.' (The Guardian, Feb 19, 2009.)

That's TRILLION with a capital T. Am I the only one who thinks this is insane?

Why should the public shoulder the real costs in debt payment over years and years just so the banks can avoid having to use their own assets to settle their own debts?

If we borrow to bail out the banks, we will not be able to borrow more for all the things that make this a civilized country. At that point, no matter how many pensions are obliterated, no matter how many people are made homeless, no matter how many unemployed there are, no matter what cuts there are in education and no matter what cuts are made to the NHS, no matter what, we will all just have to put up with it. There will simply be no money. It will all have gone to pay off the debts of the rich.

Even if the country should slide into a severe depression, the owners of the IOUs will regard them as binding. They will expect their debts to be paid no matter what tax hikes and welfare cuts are required. The government will have to convince the markets that the population will absolutely pay back. Any sign of social unrest and the market will infer a greater risk of default. Our credit rating would then go down, and the premium we have to pay would escalate. To prevent this, I believe the government would deploy the full range of state powers and forces against us, casting any talk of debt repudiation as akin to terrorism. There would be a police crackdown on the ranks of trade unionists, student protestors, community campaigners and political activists in the name of national, and even international, security.

By borrowing this money to bail out the banks, we are selling democratic control. The markets will have a veto on our vote. It has happened in developing countries for decades where many governments have simply been puppets of the IMF. Now we are going to enjoy the same status.

That is why time is running out to act now. It won't work to say, 'let's not rock the boat and see what happens.' Major civil unrest may be some way off yet, but some sort of significant protest now, even civil unrest, would be better than keeping quiet until we have been herded into a state where only extreme measures and huge disobedience can extricate us.

I have an abiding fear that the size of the debts we are being shackled to, the scale of the devastation to hopes and lives that paying it back will cause, is just not hitting people. By the time it does, I worry it will be too late. People seem to think this is still in the land of argument and counter argument. But once the debt is sold and the money used then, no matter how horrified people get when they realise the actual cost in misery and deprivation, they will no longer have the option of changing their minds.

You know the small print of any investment says, 'Returns can go down as well as up'? Well, so can freedoms.

CHAPTER 6

Non-Linear Times

24 Feb 09

Can you believe there are still idiot commentators saying this 'economic downturn' is just like others and, with time, will pass. Of course it will pass, but at what cost?

Previous downturns have not engulfed so many of the world's economies at the same time. No previous downturn has involved the disintegration of virtually all the world's major banks. The banks died some time ago but have been kept on life support by our governments pumping endless amounts of new blood into them. The problem is that blood has just seeped uselessly all over the floor. Their assets are collapsing in value by the day, and trade and consumption in the real world are spiralling down. The markets know the banks are not recovering.

The situation reminds me of the scene in Monty Python and the Holy Grail where Arthur chops off the Black Knight's arms and legs. This may not turn out to be *the* crisis of capitalism, but it sure as hell isn't just a scratch or a flesh wound.

If anyone still thinks the economic crisis we are going through is V shaped or U shaped, or in fact any other kind of textbook nonsense, just contemplate, for a minute, the state of AIG.

For those who might have forgotten, AIG *was* the world's largest insurer and the epicentre of credit default swaps and insurance. It went bust at the time Lehman Brothers collapsed. It was bailed out with tens of billions. The bailout didn't work. It went bust again. It was bailed out a second time. Total bailout so far? $150bn.

Well, it's bust yet again! This week it will declare losses of a further $60bn! It will tell the US government that it needs the $60bn by Monday, or it will collapse. No one dares imagine what would happen if it did.

AIG has been the one that has frightened them all along. The fact that they are in trouble again tells me that their assets are rotting faster and that those they owe money to are calling in the debts more aggressively. The slack is going out of the rope. The weight is pulling them back towards the edge again.

Time is running out both for Mr Obama and for us here in Europe. The markets have plunged and will continue to nose-dive until they get what they want: certainty about what is going to happen to all the bad debts that are sitting on the banks' balance sheets. This is perhaps the only question that matters.

In the US, the markets are so desperate for the banks' losses to be taken into the public debt that they are even willing to see the banks and insurers nationalised. If this happens, and the debt is taken on, then I think we are in for an even bigger problem. The size of that debt will require a level of borrowing that the debt market just will not accept. Not even the US government can nationalise *all* the debt. It would push US borrowing to levels that would, sooner or later, crush even their credit rating.

This, in turn, would presage a bigger and deeper disaster. US borrowing is already becoming increasingly geared to the short end of the curve. They have to roll over tens of billions every week. A single failure to roll it and BOOM! Sovereign default. The US is fast approaching the point where they are damned if they borrow more and damned if they don't. But that is the path we will find ourselves on because Obama and all the others are still relying on those who got us into this mess to show us the way out.

26 Feb 09

The scale of the horror show at the Royal Bank of Scotland (RBS) is gradually becoming clear. Today they announced losses of more than £24bn – the biggest loss in British corporate history. At the same time it was also announced, under Alistair Darling's scheme, that the taxpayer will be insuring £300bn of their worst assets. £300bn in insuring the same stuff that has bankrupted AIG! That's our recovery plan? Nice.

Insuring RBS's bad debts isn't a policy decision – it's plain insanity.

RBS's losses will grow beyond the present insurance agreement with the government, and everyone knows it. The insurance, as it stands right now, could be much more than is being admitted to. Others of the bailed out walking dead will follow them. HBOS is in a similar position. How much we could end up paying is anybody's guess. But, make no mistake, the money will be paid, and when it is the situation will get rapidly worse.

Our borrowing is already putting the nation's credit rating at risk. Hungary, Latvia and Ireland have already suffered downgrades. As we borrow more and more to cover the banks' debts, the risk is that we will suffer the same fate. And that will only be the beginning.

27 Feb 09

Now here is a surprise. Jean-Claude Trichet, the head of the European Central Bank, has just declared, 'We live in non-linear times …' At last! The only problem is that all the thinking of those who govern us is still entirely linear. And this is a deep part of why nothing they have done has had the effect they expected.

Our leaders and their economic masters are linear recidivists. They still think of the economy as if it were a machine that has broken down. Somewhere in its innards some fool has thrown a wrench that has lodged in vital gears and bent all sorts of rods and connectors. Brown still thinks it's something he can fix – with some help from Obama.

They imagine all they need to do is pour in lots of lubricating money, replace a few bent and busted parts, then press the big green GO button and the machine will roar back to life. Which would work if it were a linear machine. But it's not. A machine breaks down and waits innertly to be fixed. When fixed it works exactly as it did before it broke. That's the linear world.

Non-linear phenomena do not break and then wait to be put back as they were. Non-linear systems don't break, they change. They come to tipping points which mark the moment at which the system irrevocably alters. They change from one way of behaving to another, which can be quite different. Non-linear systems don't break, they mutate. The economy isn't broken: it has mutated.

Still not convinced? Take this metaphor the economists are always using: 'thaw out the credit markets'. Imagine a few years hence when all the Arctic sea ice has melted. Apply our leaders' linear thinking to this problem, and they would insist that, at vast expense, we should refreeze all the ice. Get up there with fridges and freezers and put all the ice back.

Of course, it would be futile since the system would have changed to a warmer configuration. But they would not understand this and would be surprised that their emergency measures weren't having the effect they had anticipated.

This lunacy is what we are currently engaged in with the economy.

The system is non-linear. It has passed a tipping point. It will not be put back as it was. All the vast despoiling of public finance has been in service of putting things back as they were. STOP IT. IT WON'T WORK.

1 Mar 09

Yet more mind numbing insight from the experts this morning. 'What the markets need above all else', declared one eminent commentator, 'is stability.' Wrong, wrong, wrong you silly little man. Didn't they teach you anything on your MBA? It is volatility, not stability, which markets thrive on. Volatility is why what is happening to the world today is happening. Volatility is the secret name of modern Mammon. Understand volatility and we can really see what is going on.

They would like you to think it is complicated, but it's not. It's worth a little digression to understand.

Imagine a flat, horizontal line. That represents owning a stock, share or bond – any asset. If the value of your asset stays the same as time ticks by, the line remains perfectly horizontal. Now picture the same straight line, but imagine it going up at a slight incline. That is your asset gaining in value.

Normally you would think of the profit as being how much the line has risen compared to where it was when you first bought the asset. This is where you need to adjust your thinking to understand the importance of volatility to modern trading. The height of the line, where it reaches, is indeed how much the asset is now worth. But you need to think of the profit as being measured by the length of the line. The diagonal is longer than the flat line. For as long as you own that asset, you track the diagonal line and the profit is yours.

Measuring the diagonal line is one way of understanding the old-fashioned buy and hold trading strategy. The one used by little old ladies and big fat gents. They invest in a 'good' company with 'prospects' or, better yet, a blue chip company and wait for their broker to call or their butler to bring the dividend check. They get to spend the dividend and feel warm inside looking at how much the value of their investment has risen.

By buying and holding the asset they get all the profit of that rising line. The steeper it goes up, the longer the line, the more profit you make. It's the kind of investing you do if what you do is look for the fundamentals of a company: its patents, fixed assets, cash etc. It's an easy and accurate graphic device, but it limits you. You could potentially earn a vast amount more. All you need is the magic of volatility.

Volatility is when instead of a smooth line it jigs up and down the way we have all seen the stock market index do. That jigging up and down *is* volatility. The old-fashioned way of seeing this is to dismiss it as just like interference on a radio signal. The underlying signal is the smooth average line you can draw through the zigs and zags to give you an overall picture. This is the smooth line the old lady and gent used to track their investments. These people are living in yesteryear, however, and will shortly be ruined by a world of volatility trading they do not understand.

To avoid ruination, all you have to do is notice that the zigzag line is longer than the straight, smoothed out average line. This is the key to modern trading and is why what is happening in the markets today is happening.

If you trade the smooth line, ignoring the zigzag, your line is short. If you can trade the zigzags your line is longer. But the zigzags have less to do with the intrinsic long-term qualities of the company and more to do with events and circumstances outside of the company – the sea on which the company floats. Those external events create the waves that bob your company about. Lending rates, oil costs, politicians raising the minimum wage, or a crisis in bank lending that cuts off the ability of companies to borrow money for investing in new machinery, for example.

Now, imagine you knew much less about the company itself but a lot about all these external circumstances. With a little help, you might then be able to anticipate and track some of these events. That could completely change how you trade. Instead of buying and holding – ignoring all the zigzags – you buy and sell like crazy. You sell just before the line zags down and buy back just before it zigs up. If you do that with more than 50% accuracy then the line you are following, your profit, is longer than the straight line. A lot longer.

Now you are not really investing any more. You are beginning to trade, or speculate.

Let's ramp it up. Now you don't worry about many of the details of the companies you trade at all. You have realised that all the companies, good and bad, are bobbed about by the same forces. They are all sailing on the same sea. So, being one of the smartest people in the room, rather than just do research into the companies you now research the sea and its weather. You try to get to know who and what might make waves. If you can find out before other people you will know when the zigs and zags are going to happen before others do. You will then trade those zigzags at much closer to 100% accuracy and will be hailed as a genius. (This is known as 'insider trading' to some people or 'being well connected' to others.)

Now you are a fully-fledged speculator. The closer you can track that chaotic, zigzag line the more money you will make. And that profit will be much greater than the profit you could possibly have achieved from simply tracking the smooth average rise. Sit down and enjoy a glass of Bolly because you have just helped bring about one of the most significant revolutions in modern times. Profit is now no longer identical with value! Bravo!

This becomes even clearer when you realise that you can make profit from the stock going down. You sell some assets. After you sell them, those assets then decline in value. You buy them back at this lower price. The value then goes back up to where it was. Overall the value has not altered, but you are richer! Magic? No, short selling. Read it again, it works. I promise.

Let's go even further. You now no longer buy anything tangible at all. Instead, you take bets with someone on which way the line of value will go. You can bet on it zigging up, or you can bet on it zagging down. Now you are trading in derivatives and credit default swaps. Congratulations. Order yourself a whole crate of Bolly and an even bigger house because you've deserved it.

I have been talking in terms of assets, rather than just shares, for a reason. The reason is that debt is traded in exactly the same way. No one buys and holds debt: they trade it. The value of debt goes up and down. It is volatile. If the markets can create debt volatility by, let's say, speculating on default using credit default swap bets then they can track and trade that misery for profit. Well done! Buy yourself another house or maybe a yacht.

Now, you just need to notice one more thing. If you get out a magnifying glass, you will see that every zigzag has smaller zigzags embedded in it. Like a fractal, the line has more detail as you magnify it. By magnifying the line you are in effect looking at smaller and smaller time scales. As with fractals, what you suddenly realise, as they did in the 1980s, is that as you magnify the line it grows longer. There is, in fact, much more of the line in these tiny little wiggles than the human eye can see or track.

But, imagine if you were superhuman and could move fast enough to track all those changes – buy and sell each and every one. Of course, the changes are tiny fractions of value, but there are thousands of them packed into every second of every day. If you can trade them all, and stay on the right side of the line, then you are on your way to becoming very rich indeed. All you need, apart from being inhumanly fast, is to be rich enough to buy a million shares to start you off. Then a hundredth of a dollar change in value on a million shares has made you a thousand dollars in a microsecond.

All it needed was the invention of the computer and a few whiz-kid programmers to build machine-trading computers and away you go. Congratulations again. Now you are a High Frequency Trader (HFT).

And that's what modern markets do: they trade the volatile zigs and zags of the line. They need volatility. They make it. They get others to make it for them. They try to get inside knowledge of who will make what waves. Those who get to know 'front-run' events. They cheat.

Now, volatility is fine when it is relatively tame. It's like a wind that fills the sails. But if the storm is too violent, you can sink. High frequency trading computers are brilliant at tracking the tiny flickerings of the line. The danger is that the machines cannot see larger zigzags. So when a really large zig hits them they glitch. The machines either sell, and track the sell down to stay ahead of it, or they simply shut down, and a vast chunk of the market's liquidity disappears. Either one is not good for everyone else and sends all *their* computers into an automated frenzy. What makes all this so dangerous is that it happens at a speed no human can even see, let alone stop.

Volatility is what makes the world go up and down! It's what makes them money. It is also what can kill them.

But volatility isn't just a product of computers: it's also a product of the people who use them. Just as the revolution in modern financial thinking separated profit from value, so there has been a parallel revolution in thinking about what it actually means to make and lose money.

Losing money used to be a simple measure of how much you have now compared to how much you had before. Any decrease and you had lost. Those were gentle times; ours are not.

Today you can have officially lost money even if you made a profit and are richer. This new, high pressure 'losing money' is part of what is driving the volatility in the markets. Losing is now no longer measured against the static yardstick of what you had before. It is now measured against the moving target of what the person who made the very most earned.

Let's say you make x. If the whiz-kid who has his eye on your job makes twice that amount, then the difference between what you could have made and what you actually did make is the magnitude of your failure as a trader. Despite making a profit you are now, in the eyes of your boss, officially a LOSER.

This is now how finance works. The City advertises its 'star' investors and fund managers. It shouts the percentage their fund could make you. It sneers at all those who made less. The fact that they actually made a profit dissolves under the acid comparison with what they should have made if they weren't LOSERS.

And this is why the City chases risk and abuses leverage like they were drugs. It is a matter of personal and company survival. How are you going to be the all-conquering banker, commanding the huge bonus if you make less than some other rising star? You won't be. How will your hedge fund make the A-list if it doesn't perform up there with the best returns anyone has ever seen? It won't.

Of course, the corrective to this was supposed to be the sobering and steadying possibility that you would overreach. You would take a risk too far, stretch your leverage too thin and become that modern day leper: a rogue trader! This was the City fable of self-regulation and the natural corrective mechanisms of the market. Experience has shown, over and over again, that it is about as reliable and terrifying as the threat of Greek income tax.

Previously the failure of these corrective, 'self-regulatory mechanisms' were glossed over as the workings of 'animal spirits' or 'irrational optimism'. As if crash after crash, scandal after scandal, dotcom burst after tech bubble bust, were all some sort of, boys will be boys, high jinx to be overlooked and tolerated as a necessary part of life.

Then, when the big bust came, after an orgy of risk and idiocy to end all orgies, finally the bankers discovered the answer: too big to fail. Now there is no threat of loss at all. Now they can take any risk they want and if it goes wrong just shriek and scream that the world is going to end until they are given another bailout. Losing money is now something only taxpayers do.

The problem facing everyone, however, is that even the debts national governments can incur to bail out these losses is not limitless. At some point, there won't be enough money even to give to the bankers.

And this, I believe, is where we are now. Our economy is being driven by drunken boy racers at 100 mph who have just had a massive blow-out. They are so drunk they refuse all advice to pull over or even to just slow down. They tell us they don't even need to replace the tyre. All we need to do is frantically pump in new air while we are still careering along, swinging wildly all over the road.

To me, in such a situation, there only seem to be two options: either they wreck the car and we all get hurt – a bond market dislocation – or we, the passengers, overcome our fear and fight to seize control of the car. At the moment, I think we are on course to wreck the car and then have a huge fight afterwards. The worst of both worlds.

2 Mar 09
It's all kicking off today. HSBC, the world's third largest bank, put out an urgent call for £12.5bn in cash today after announcing it had lost over $15bn through its US mortgage subsidiary Household International.

Why did HSBC's losses take until now to surface? What it says to me is that its US subsidiary Household International made loans to slightly more creditworthy people than those classed as subprime. I think this means the collapse in housing has now spread up from subprime, which means that the 'better' tranches of securities and derivatives, mezzanine and senior, once thought to be safe, will soon go underwater.

And then take a look at General Electric (GE). It's getting shorted to the ground. This is ominous. Not that they don't deserve it. GE is leveraged way over 100. Even Citigroup is only 60 something. I think this is the market betting on a ratings downgrade. And just look at what is happening with credit default swaps on GE's debt. The markets are asking for payment up front. That is exactly what they asked for with both Bear Stearns' and Lehmans' debt just before they went BOOM! What this means is that the markets now regard non-bank finance as bankrupt. GE is being shorted because GE Capital, its financial arm, is feared dead in the water just like GMAC, the financial arm of General Motors. The fear is they may be going down soon, and, if they do, it won't stop there.

How serious might this be? Well GE Capital is one of the biggest non-bank financial institutions. If GE Capital goes, AIG won't survive either. One goes, they both go. If that happens, it's all over. The cascade would then be unstoppable.

AIG knew this. According to a story by Andrew Ross Sorkin in the New York Times, AIG have been circulating a 'strictly confidential' report to US regulators. The report, AIG: Is the Risk Systemic, claims: 'The failure of AIG would cause turmoil in the US economy and global markets and have multiple and potentially catastrophic consequences.' It goes on to say that, compared to Lehman Brothers, 'the government would be even less capable of predicting the fallout from a much larger, more global and more consumer orientated institution such as AIG.'

This is *after* they have already had over $160bn. And, believe me, they are not exaggerating their importance.

If all that isn't enough, take a look at Citigroup. Once called the world's largest bank, their shares are now selling for UNDER $1. Read that again, and let it sink in.

HSBC's losses, GE, including GE Capital, being attacked and maybe getting downgraded, AIG still haemorrhaging and Citigroup hanging by a thread. All this makes me think we are as close to the cliff's edge now as we were when Lehman Brothers went down.

5 Mar 09

Now a new phase of the crisis really does get underway. After lots of talk, Mervyn King is announcing today that the Bank of England is going to officially start the printing presses and 'quantitatively ease' tens of billions into the economy.

Of course, he is not going to do that by loading a helicopter full of £10 notes and dropping them over London in the hope that people will spend it in the nearest shop. He is trying to do the same thing by a slightly more circuitous route. What he is going to do is use the new money to buy up government gilts from the banks holding them. The hope is that the banks will suddenly feel free to start splashing their new cash round the economy in the form of loans to companies and consumers.

Brown, King and the rest of the ideologues believe that such is the deflationary vacuum being created by the destruction of asset value that they can print into this vacuum without risk of inflation. But they ignore a vital question: will the bond market want to buy our debt once we start inflating the money supply? If they see us buying our own debt with newly printed money, they may begin to question the future value of that debt.

The bond market could slow down or even stop buying our IOUs due to worries that their value may be inflated away. If they do keep buying, we could see the cost begin to ramp up significantly to factor in the increased risk of inflation. Speculators could also see quantitative easing in a weak economy like ours as a green light to move against the pound and pound denominated debt.

I sincerely fear that with QE what happened to the banks could happen to the country. We are now facing the real possibility of both a run on the pound and a credit downgrade on our national debt. All this in a doomed attempt to save a rotting financial system now beyond salvation.

For those in doubt take note. Foreign investors pulled £700bn of their money *out* of the City of London in the last half of last year. I'd say that might be an indication that they don't believe the UK can sustain the debt it is taking on.

Our 'free market', global trade infatuated leaders talk a lot about the need to avoid nationalism and protectionism of goods, but they haven't yet twigged that the real nationalism and protectionism is in money, not goods. Money is heading home. Capital is where the new protectionism will be. I think we will see growing evidence of sovereign funds and foreign central banks in China, Japan and the oil nations decreasing their debt buying in other countries. Not 'our jobs for our workers', but 'our bailout money for our problems'. China will spend more of its money on its internal problems. The US is already heading in that direction. Only Brown is still banging the drum for his failed vision of globalism. King Canute springs to mind.

And then there is oil. The entire logic of the financial bailout is based on very low oil prices keeping inflation non-existent.

Oil shot up. Oil crashed down. Only an idiot looks at the present price and sees it as a stable indicator of future price levels. What we have is extreme price volatility. So what will happen to our bailouts and massive public debt when oil goes back up – as it will? We could easily find ourselves servicing vast levels of debt while watching in horror as inflation returns. Nice plan boys!

14 Mar 09

Despite what Brown and King are hoping for, I think we're going to see lots more market volatility in the coming weeks. Their liquidity injections, and those in the States, have got so much cash sloshing around the system that volatility is going to increase, not decrease. That's going to mean fast ups and even faster downs.

Of course, some of that money will be looking for safety, which means buying government debt, but there will be a huge amount looking to find a quick profit anyway it can.

I think we will see this search for a quick profit increasingly boiling down to fronting government bailouts and shorting. There is definitely money to be made by investing just before, or straight after, the announcement of government bailouts. You then ride the pop up and sell a bit later to those a little slower off the mark. As for shorting, I think it will become even more predatory.

Short selling, like many things in the financial world, can seem to be extremely complicated, but it's not. It is essentially borrowing shares, for a fee, with an agreement to return them on a specified date. The short seller then sells those shares. He does so because he is betting that the share price will go down. If he is correct, then when the price does go down he can buy the same shares back at the lower price. He then returns them to the original owner, as agreed, and pockets the difference between the price he sold at and the lower price he repurchased them for. Clever.

Naked shorting just leaves out actually borrowing the shares. This means you can place your bet on which way the share price is going to go without actually having to go to the inconvenience of buying any shares at all. This way you can make far larger bets far more often. You can, therefore, potentially make huge profits because you can make a bet on any number of shares you fancy – a huge company crippling number if you want, and no one, not even the actual owners of the stock, can stop you.

Critically, placing those bets feeds back into the real market for those shares. A lot of bets against a share price make people think something is up. They therefore sell, and the price does go down. This is why people claim naked shorting speculatively drives prices down. And indeed it does. Big players can make a price go down by frightening the market. And that, I believe, is what we are going to see. Lots of ups and lots of downs thanks to all the extra cash our governments are pumping into the banks.

In effect, all they are doing by putting in so much extra cash is to smother the real conditions in the global market. But the real, underlying problems haven't disappeared. They are still there unaddressed and as dangerous as they were. Only now, they are submerged in a sloshing, spilling mess.

23 Mar 09

For the past week the market has been on an up, and everyone has started to talk as if the crisis was on the mend. There have even been articles about, 'how to prevent this happening again', as if this crisis were over and done with. IT ISN'T!

This crisis has only ever been about debt and insolvency, not about stock prices. People are so fixated by what the stock market is doing they think a rise in the index heralds the Second Coming. They are wrong.

What we are experiencing is a rerun of the rally we had in November of last year. It lasted a month. Then the markets crashed another 200 points.

Rises in stock prices, particularly in financials, do not mean traders see a sign of recovery: it means they see a quick, short-term profit to be made. The rise in financial stocks is simply speculative. You front-run a rumour and then sell before the bubble bursts.

The stock prices are like the patient's temperature. You can use it to gauge how sick he is, but it isn't the cause of the illness. You can bring the temperature down, pack him in ice, give him fluids, but if the virus is untreated he's still sick and may well die. All this liquidity pumped into the system has only ever treated the symptoms. For reasons we can all speculate upon, the bankers and their servants have stonewalled any discussion, let alone action, to deal with the festering cause of the sickness: the debts.

I believe the stock market has rallied because the banks see they are going to make money unloading bad assets under the plan just announced by the new secretary of the US Treasury, Timothy Geithner. And why wouldn't they? Look at the plan.

The US government will loan 85% of the money to buyers of the banks' assets. Of the remaining 15%, the US Treasury will actually put up 95% itself. The only collateral the buyer has to put up is the rubbish he's buying. This means the buyer runs almost no risk at all courtesy of the US taxpayer. And there will be lots of takers. If, by some miracle, the assets do well then the buyer profits. If they continue to rot, what has the buyer lost? Virtually nothing. Heads they win, tails we lose! Nice! That's what they call private money helping out.

So let's ignore the artificially induced temperature of the stock market. The real indicator of the underlying infection has always been in the bond markets. The proof of this is that at the same time that stocks were ramping up the spread on bonds was also increasing.

What does that mean? It says that while speculators are looking for profits from short-term ups and downs, the bond market is pricing in a very large medium and long-term decline. The bond market is looking at the balance sheet, and what they see are still massive undeclared losses.

The signs are in the spreads of insuring debt of all kinds. Spreads on corporate debt are widening and, most worryingly, so are those on sovereign debt. The bond market is saying, loud and clear, that there is much worse to come. That's why China has been making ominous noises about wanting the US to protect China's $1 trillion plus holdings of dollar debt. Last week there was a net selling of US debt. A small net selling, but it's still very significant at a time when the US needs to sell so much new debt.

To me, all this points to the stock markets taking another lurch down in the not too distant future. If there is no substantive agreement out of the G20, and I don't think there will be, then that could well trigger a big fall. If it doesn't happen in the few days after the G20 then I give it until late summer at the very latest.

At that point, I think the markets will fall over again, and we'll be on another downward slide. That larger lurch down could well be the point that civil unrest will take off because no amount of talk will cover over the fact that all the bailouts haven't worked. We will have spent all the money on their plans and there will be nothing left. No more borrowing, as Mr King pointed out, to pay for everything that makes this country a decent place to live.

25 Mar 09

What many of us have been fearing for a while happened today. The government auction of its debt failed to find enough bidders. If this happens a second time, the UK is holed beneath the water line.

Our options then would be few. We could ditch the pound and issue our debt in euros. We could offer such a yield on our gilts that they would at least sell, even if they bankrupted us further down the line. Or we could make such savage cuts in spending from health to pensions and education that we don't need to borrow more.

All of the above spell one thing to me: huge social unrest.

Last year we learnt how politics is ruled by economics. This year we will learn the lesson on the other side of the coin. That economics gets pretty bloody political when people get hungry, homeless and frightened.

30 Mar 09

Up we went, down we go. Stock markets around the world had steep falls today on news that the US car industry may go bankrupt.

It just shows that the bankers and their servants, the politicians, have learnt nothing. For two weeks there's a rally in stocks and, in their world, they are kings again and can strut around telling us little people to get back in our boxes.

But this was not a recovery. It was the brief re-animation of a corpse for the sole profit of the bankers and speculators. How was it achieved? The US used AIG to funnel massive amounts of US taxpayers' money to the major banks – a bailout without the negative press. Goldman alone got $12.9bn. It went into AIG and straight back out to Goldman. This allowed the banks to seem flush. Just like pumping blood into a corpse can make it look pink. The money gave the banks a blush of health and relieved them of an imminent crisis. The speculators saw a chance for quick money, our money, and took it. Literally.

The rally of the last two weeks was never solid. Not a recovery. The fact supporting this is that the news about General Motors' possible bankruptcy has been enough to fling the markets into reverse again.

And there is a triple whammy for the markets in that news.

First, the shock to General Motors' management, and their bankers, that the company may not be too big to fail. This is a shocker, *par excelence*, because becoming too big to fail has been the main survival strategy of the banks. That it might not work would be a death sentence for the likes of Wells Fargo and Bank of America. Then there is the massive effect on employment and manufacturing if General Motors were to go. Such a move would pull down a whole supply chain including every one from rolled steel suppliers to makers of speciality parts. Bankruptcy for the car giant would also bring down its financial arm GMAC, which would, in turn, bring down the people who own the other half of GMAC, Cerberus Capital. Then, last but by no means least, there is the effect on the bond market. There are so many credit default swaps written on General Motors' debt that for them to default would be huge. All this would come at a time when the major debts of other big companies are also falling over.

This was never about a recovery. Our politicians are lost. They are too afraid and too in thrall to the emperors of finance to see that the massive losses must be cleared from the system and taken by those who made them. Sadly, the only future that Brown and the economic pundits can imagine is making all of us pay off the debts for a system that will be nothing but a workhouse, where we and our children labour to pay the gambling bills of the rich.

I do think civil unrest is now inevitable. I didn't think so at first. I hoped, more than believed, that there might be some possibility of escaping the mental straightjacket of bailout dogma. But the failure of imagination of our political leadership has been utter and complete. They are leading us to a desperate place.

CHAPTER 7

The Train Divides

31 Mar 09

For anyone who has never been 'kettled' it is when the police at a protest suddenly close ranks and refuse to let anyone leave. You suddenly find you are held against your wishes. The police will not explain why, and they won't allow any exceptions. You suddenly have no control over what is happening, and no discussion is permitted. A decision made by someone you have never seen now exerts complete and total control over your life.

We are all in that position now.

So vast is the debt our government has burdened us with that this one fact will now determine most of the politics of the next decade. Other hopes and desires – the wish for better schools, a better health service, better care for the elderly – will wither in the shadow of the debt repayments. If we are forced to pay back from taxes all the vast sums that have been sucked out of public spending and given to the banks, the country will not recover for a generation.

The economic 'plans', forced on us without debate, are all based on the banks returning large parts of the money they have taken from us. This means, whether we like it or not, we all have to hope that the banks make profits as quickly as possible. We have all been 'kettled' into having to hope and work for the largest possible growth in world trade and finance. We have to hope that the rich get richer, and quickly. The lords of finance and their servants in politics decided this for us.

There never was any discussion or debate of possible alternatives when the financial crisis began. It was declared, and universally agreed (always a bad sign), that the problem was liquidity, not solvency. That meant the only answer ever proposed was to provide liquidity at all costs. Liquidity being *our* money to cover the massive losses *they* had incurred. This, we were told, wasn't really a cost at all, but 'an investment'. An investment which would pay back all the loaned, borrowed and printed money long before the debts came due through reinflated levels of growth and asset value.

That was, and is, their only plan. And so absolute is the certainty in the minds of all concerned that none of them can even conceive of looking beyond the closed circle of that logic. No counter-argument is allowed or taken seriously. No warning signs are read as such.

Their so-called 'free market' has seized control and locked us in to a course of action in which democratic choice has been foreclosed. The growing realisation that this is what is happening will bring about increased anger. The smug reaction to anger is to label it 'mindless'. The mindless anger of the ignorant who don't understand the necessary steps being taken by those who know better. That is the boiled down assumption of all our leaders, all the economic experts and most economic journalists.

The truth is quite different. People like me are angry because exactly the same people who, in 2008, assumed they knew how to run the global economy still assume they, and only they, know what must be done now. And their prescription is as simple as it is arrogant: put it back the way it was.

We are told that the debts accrued by those in charge must be paid by us rather than honoured by them. No debate.

We are told we must get lending back to the old levels. No debate.

We are told we must get the consumer consuming again rather than saving. No debate.

We are told that we must agree and complete the Doha round of global free trade liberalization. No debate.

To be robbed is one thing: to be condescended to by the people who robbed you is another altogether.

That is why many people like me are angry. We are angry because the financial elite are shoving their ideology down our throats. We are angry because we might have wanted to have a say. We are angry because we had different ideas that were never even considered.

Here we are at the point in history when many of us are looking at the imminent threats of climate change and oil scarcity, clearly seeing the dangers of unbridled growth, and yet at this point democratic choice has been kettled. No debate.

And that is why this crisis is no longer just about lack of confidence in the markets: it is now about the legitimacy of our governments. The entire political class has been captured by the same ideology. They all, to one extent or another, believe 'the market' is going to save us. No other solutions have even been allowed into the debate.

We shouldn't waste our time arguing over which party is most to blame. All the parties and the economists and the

City boys all agreed, and they still do. In their minds the banks had to be bailed out and their losses made ours. We were taken to war without discussion and on false pretences; the same has happened with this financial crisis. So enough of who is to blame: they all were and are.

They all believe in a system that says we must create demand and then feed it with debt. This necessarily involves increasing demand by the creation of yet more debt. It always crashes and always will. That is how their system works. If we allow it to be the solution, it will create another crash and another. Each time the rich will reap profits on the way up and rape the public purse on the way down. It's win, win for them and lose, lose for us. *Plus ça change!*

2 Apr 09

News our leaders would like me to be cheering came today as shares rallied again on the back of hopes that the G20 leaders meeting in London will resolve their differences.

No one can tell for sure how long this current rally will hold. Our leaders hope it will gather enough momentum to lift the burden of debts. I think it is more of a hope than a real plan. But, whatever the case, it doesn't change the fact that the infection still has a tight grip on debts and bonds. And that infection is still spreading.

Let's just see what happens to General Motors and, more importantly, to the credit default swaps written on its bonds. There are a few, very cogent commentators who are betting that AIG will end up being behind many of GM's credit default swap positions. If so, the fate of GM and AIG could collide much like a star colliding with a black hole: the one ripping the other apart releasing killing forces that sterilize all life around the event horizon.

I, personally, have no insight into how likely this is beyond the facts that AIG loved to write credit default swaps, and a lot were written on GM bonds. It does, however, reinforce what I have been arguing for a while: that the place to look is not the stock market. The seat of the infection has always been in the debt and the bond market.

13 Apr 09

The head of the Fed, Ben Bernanke, has just said he saw 'tentative signs' that the US economy may be on the road to recovery. Part of his optimism came from financial results from Goldman Sachs, which, on paper at least, showed quarterly profits of $1.66bn.

Let's look at Goldman's figures in a little more detail. Could their profits be anything to do with the suspension of mark-to-market accounting? I wonder. Hmmm.

Come on folks, look what happened. Goldman gets lots of Fed cash on the quiet via AIG. They then get another shed load direct from the US government's Troubled Asset Relief Program (TARP). Finally, with the suspension of mark-to-market, Goldman and the others can pretend their assets are worth whatever they want. Blimey. Even I could be worth a billion with those sort of rules.

Goldman's figures are a pump and dump. Buy at your peril. I'm not saying there isn't a rally to ride for a while, but it's hot air driven and when the bubble cools gravity takes over and its straight down at 9.8m/s/s.

Rather than look at Goldman's make believe figures, let's look at some real world economics like the implosion of commercial real estate. This morning General Growth Properties, one of the largest commercial real estate operators in the US, filed for bankruptcy. They collapsed when they couldn't finance $25bn in loans. Other will follow.

If that isn't enough, you have a new wave of residential mortgages defaults about to hit. Just as subprime has worked its way through the system, now defaults on the mortgages above them, Alt-A and Option ARM, are up between 10 and 20% in suburbs. It's what the charts said would happen over a year ago and, bang on time, here it comes. Residential foreclosures jumped last month as a moratorium on them ended.

Why bathe in all this misery rather than listen to the siren call of those who say it's all getting better? Because their false counsel is what has led us to make so many disastrous decisions. They said the banks could be bailed out and that we could afford it. Both were lies, and lies that will hurt us for a generation.

Please stop believing the fraudsters and the ideologically blinded!

14 Apr 09

All those now talking about 'green shoots' should spend less time getting over-excited about short-term rallies in the stock market and spend more time looking at the flow of money upon which their 'recovery' will ultimately depend.

Are you looking at what the quants are doing, particularly Goldman? Seems to me if you are serious about green shoots you should look hard at this story. That gives a far more accurate picture of what is happening with this current rally.

Quant trading is the trading by computer programmes run mostly by the primary dealer banks and a few specialist houses. It's the type of trading that deals with the minute, volatile zigzags invisible to the naked eye. The trades they make are pure speculation. They don't buy for underlying value, and they don't hold what they buy. They make money by buying and selling fast, getting tiny profits on shifting millions of shares. If this is a quant driven rally, it would suggest that it is *not* based on any real improvement in the underlying profitability of the companies whose shares are being traded.

Goldman is, according to the most recent figures from the New York Stock Exchange (NYSE), by far the largest quant trader. It's five times larger by volume than anyone else. People who watch this market closely are getting more than a little twitchy. The suspicion is that the big quant traders could be shifting shares around between themselves, giving the impression of desirability, and thus driving the prices up. Even the Chief Executive of the NYSE has voiced his concern.

If real money, real value traders, day-time traders, begin to really buy into the rally (it hasn't happened so far) then the rally becomes 'real' and self-sustaining. But, for this to happen, there will have to be solid evidence from earnings, orders and consumption data that make the real money boys and girls believe earnings will increase and bankruptcies go down.

If this rally is a sucker rally, and if it has been driven by quant trading at the margins and over-night, we will know in the next two months tops. If it is all hot air then when it cools we would then see a sharp liquidity contraction and a big fall in prices. That will signal the next sharp leg down.

What I don't understand is why anyone is being fooled and parted from their money by this rally? At the moment, I find incredulity and disbelief build up like wind, and you either have to let it out or feel ill with it all.

16 Apr 09

As I have said before, it's the bond market we need to watch, not the stock market. The latest figures are showing something very interesting.

There is a very marked slowing in the amount of US debt the Chinese are buying. The best I can make out is that the Chinese may even have begun to off-load a small amount of their total holdings. But this decrease is not the real story. The real story is more interesting than that.

If China simply began to sell their holdings, both they and the US would implode. The two countries are locked in a death embrace. Each needs the other to do well. Neither wants the other to fail. America needs China to buy its debt and China needs America to be able to pay it back. A dollar collapse hurts them both.

What China and other major buyers of US debt are doing is stopping altogether buying long-dated debt in favour of two to three-year debt. It is a way of reducing their exposure without being seen to be selling outright. This is clever. If you hold long-dated debt (20-30 yrs), you are at the mercy of inflation and other catastrophes. But with short-term debt, which gets repaid in two to three years, you are much safer, and you hold the debtor buy the balls.

The more short-term debt the US has, the more it has to roll over. Long-term debt leaves you free in the 20-30 years of the debt agreement to do what you want. With short-term debt your creditors are always looking over your shoulder. Always saying, 'Hmm, I'm not sure if I like you doing that.' It gives you a nasty feeling of not being master in your own house. It also gives the creditor much more political leverage. If China doesn't like what Obama does, they just don't reinvest when their three-year treasuries mature. This means the US government had better listen carefully to what they say.

Make no mistake, it is a very significant change.

17 Apr 09

This morning Citigroup announced profits for the first quarter at $1.6bn, almost identical to Goldman Sachs. According to some of the papers this is 'fuelling hope that Wall Street's credit crisis may be easing.'

Well, let's look at Citigroup's profits in a little more detail. Citigroup's debt is currently trading a few cents on the dollar. A terrible sign you might think. But no! Citigroup is allowed to say, 'Hmm... this means if we were to buy back our own debt on the open market, it would cost us a lot less today than it would have done three months ago. We can therefore count this as a profit!'

And, abracadabra, this clever three-card trick accounts for nearly all of the profit they claimed!

When the banks do this our lick-spittle politicians punch their air in triumph and declare, 'Job done! Crisis over!' Does anyone want to tell me that these idiots have learnt anything at all about how the system really works?

The truth is that such tricks can cover up some problems, for a while, but they can't stop commercial property from collapsing and companies like General Growth Properties going spectacularly bankrupt. Nor can accounting card tricks stop Chrysler from going down (which they will if Fiat walks away should the unions not bend over for them.)

What our leaders don't seem to realise is that the real crisis hasn't been solved: it has only just been created.

21 Apr 09

Back in Britain, Alistair Darling is to give his budget tomorrow and is talking about his 'confidence' in a recovery. In many ways, his situation reminds me of a boxer who has just received a knockout punch but has yet to fall. Often, at that moment, the fighter's hands are still up, his eyes still open. He stands like an ox, becalmed. He is on the verge of unconsciousness. That is Darling.

After the first shock of the Wall Street Crash of 1929 there was a brief period when there was a moment of calm. All the moneymen agreed the worst was over. They were wrong then; they are wrong now.

Is the government going to be able to keep financing rising unemployment as well as bailing out the banks, again, while tax receipts contract like never before?

Is the consumer going to suddenly start taking out loans despite rising unemployment and record personal debt?

Is the latest stock market rally going to claw the Dow Jones back up thousands of points?

Is property going to gain 30%, and more, to make good the other trillion plus in largely worthless mortgage-backed securities?

Oh, and that's before the Chinese fret, more than they already are doing, about the value of their dollar holdings. Have I got all the good news and positive indicators about right?

Sod confidence! You know what Alistair? I'm not a child. I object to being condescended to. How about talking to me like a grown up? Any chance?

No I thought not. Well, you can whistle for my vote.

22 Apr 09

Today we got Darling's long-awaited budget. The figures are more fatuous and laughable than I imagined. I wish people would stop listening to him. This is a man who only a year ago said the deficit would be £38bn. It's now £175bn. Why listen to a man who gets it wrong by over 400%?

His whole useless plan and predictions are based on an estimate of the likely effect of the government stimulus. That, in turn, is based on a 'multiplier effect' of how many pounds worth of growth will flow from a single pound of government spending.

I wish I could tell you that the multiplier effect is a deep piece of knowledge, but it's not. It is not based on any empirical evidence at all. It does not even have a very strong theoretical justification, which makes it rather like the rest of economic theory.

The multiplier effect Darling and the Treasury are basing their green shoots recovery on is simply a number they put into their model which is based on almost nothing more than wishful thinking.

Try it yourself. X is the money you put into the economy, the stimulus. The number you decide to multiply it by is the multiplier effect. This will tell you how much growth and recovery you are going to get. Shall we have 2x, 3x, 4x.... go on, you pick a number. It will have about as much justification as the one the Treasury picks.

Listening to these politicians is almost as daft as listening to bankers. They excuse what they tell us on the grounds that the truth is either 'hard to estimate' or would 'undermine confidence'. Being a grown-up I don't appreciate either excuse. Alistair Darling is drowning. £60bn to cover banking losses? Does anyone really believe that?

Darling and the Treasury must know that the assets underlying many more securities held by the banks and many more of their loans are going to go bad in the next two years.

Just look at what is happening in the US. Latest figures show that there are about $1.7trillion of commercial real estate loans held directly on the books of the banks and insurance companies that are now in trouble. The loans are in trouble because the value of the properties for which they were given has crashed in value. They are seriously 'underwater' or, as we say here, in negative equity.

The big problem is that commercial loans aren't for 25 years. The whole loan is for five years or so. A vast amount, about $1.4 trillion, comes due between 2010 and 2013. So far, many of the properties these loans cover have lost 35-50% of the value they had at the top of the market. By the time these loans mature, around 60% or more of the loans will be negative. With companies in so much difficulty and likely to default, the banks are going to take a huge hit.

And then there are the securities based on those loans. According to figures from the Fed, total commercial mortgage-backed securities outstanding are valued at $2.5 trillion. No one knows how much the banks have already written-down, but the best estimate is very little. This means a percentage *will* get marked down. We can get a clue as to how much by looking at what happened in residential mortgages.

Last October AA residential mortgage-backed securities (MBS) were trading at 63 cents on the dollar. They are now trading at, wait for it, 13 cents on the dollar. Even AAA residential MBS, which are backed by the Fed itself, are only trading at 25 cents on the dollar.

If a similar level of devaluation happens to commercial, and there is no good reason to suppose it won't, then this tells us, quite clearly and unambiguously, that most of the $2.5 trillion commercial mortgage-backed securities market will be wiped out. That would be double the total losses so far.

This means the banks will need to raise yet more capital. I simply cannot see them *not* returning for more bailout money. And since we have insured several hundred billion of these assets, we are on the hook to pay out. In short, *our* losses, and what we will have to borrow to cover them, are going to be much more than Darling's pathetic figures. £60bn indeed!

For those still tempted to believe that they can see green shoots from their bedroom windows, think again. This whole furore will be swept away by events sooner rather than later.

30 Apr 09

Uh, oh! The real economy looks like it is having another go at gate-crashing Brown and Obama's fancy dress party. General Motors have just announced plans to lay off another 23,000 workers. Didn't anyone tell them they were meant to come dressed as green shoots?

Will it get worse? Oh yes it will. Take a look at US Steel, the next link upstream from the carmakers. US Steel has just announced a first quarter loss and slashed its dividend by 83%. More significantly, they are having to issue $18m of new shares and $300m in new debt bonds in order to pay off outstanding debt it doesn't have the money to cover. Dilute the shareholders, run at a loss, and issue new debt to pay off old debt you can't afford. Does that sound like a recipe for recovery to you, or the road that led us to this disaster in the first place?

Get over the shock people; there is more to come, and soon.

5 May 09

Despite all the grim economic news, the latest stock market rally is giving me cause for thought. I would love to agree with those who say this is a sucker rally. After all, I have argued the same for a while now, and the rally does fly in the face of every economic fact. But let me offer a different reading. What if this rally is about politics, not economics?

Let me try to explain what I mean. There was a moment when the market players were not sure if the governments could, or would, support them. People were shocked and angry, and for a moment it even seemed possible that governments' allegiance to their economic masters was wavering. As long as there was a chance that governments might not fully backstop the losses of the major players then the market slid. The possible meltdown in financial debts was a sword of Damocles hanging over everything and everybody. While it was perceived that the debt might be forced into the market, no one felt safe. Remove that threat, and there is a feeling that the dangerous moment of doubt is behind them.

From their point of view, it makes sense to rally even if the real economy is falling apart and mass unemployment opens its jaws because their debts are covered no matter what happens to everyone else.

Don't get me wrong, I think what has been done is the largest looting of public wealth since the Enclosure Acts. I think the banks are insolvent and hiding the real truth about their debts. I think their assets are worthless and more defaults and losses are coming. I think there should be civil unrest and disobedience. But what does any of that matter if the governments have guaranteed the banks' and the markets' losses with our taxes?

But it's not just the reason for the current stock market rally that is of interest. I think it may also be pointing to something that, if true, has profound implications for all our futures. Is it possible we are seeing a decoupling of the financial economy from the rest of the economy?

Look at what is happening. Stocks, led by the banks, are rallying, but this is taking place despite an ongoing landslip in the rest of the economy with manufacturing collapsing, unemployment rising and government debt soaring out of control. Are the two parts of economy becoming fundamentally disconnected?

If so, this puts governments in a serious bind. They know that at sometime they will have to withdraw the stimulus money and raise rates to prevent inflation. But if the two parts of the economy decouple, they will end up having to withdraw the stimulus to reign in financial recovery at the same time as the real economy is still dying. Put these two thing together, and you get a picture of extreme volatility pulling in opposite directions at different times scales in different parts of the economy.

Have any of you ever watched a coupled pendulum? That's a swinging pendulum with another pendulum attached to it at the bottom. It is the mathematical model of a loosely coupled system. It is a severely chaotic system. The coupled pendulum swings wildly with the two parts wrenching at each other in ways that make both parts more unpredictable and violent.

Is it possible that we are seeing this happening with the economy? Are we witnessing a decoupling of the financial economy from the rest of the economy with the attendant unpredictable and violent results?

6 May 09

More evidence of a possible decoupling in the economy comes today.

The US government has just told Bank of America to raise $33bn more capital to deal with the worsening economic situation. But, for those who remember, it was only a month ago that Bank of America reported a $4.2bn profit. This was greeted with loud cheers at the time as a sign of real green shoots pushing through.

Unsurprisingly, not all the profit was quite what it seemed. They sold off some of their shares in China Construction Bank, nothing wrong with that. But the rest, $2.2bn, came from a clever bit of accounting. They simply increased the value of the assets they acquired last quarter when they bought Merrill Lynch. Are the assets worth more? Well no, not if they had to sell them on the open market. But they don't. Bank of America can just claim they are worth a lot more and book the difference as profit. And that's how, only a few weeks after announcing these large profits, we find they urgently need to raise $33bn. But there is something even stranger.

When a bank whose market capital base is $69bn has to raise $33bn to stay alive its shares ought to drop like a stone, but they haven't. Their bondholders ought to be selling, but they're not. Why not? Simple. They know bank debt now comes with the full 100% guarantee of the US Treasury. Their money is safer than it has ever been courtesy of the US taxpayer.

Now compare General Motors and Chrysler with Bank of America. GM has just filed its restructuring plan. It shows that shareholders will have the worth of their shares diluted down to one hundredth of their present value. So a share worth $1.85 will be worth less than two cents. Ouch! GM's bondholders are to get only 10 cents on their dollar of debt. And importantly, this is true for *senior* debt. Double ouch!

This is important because senior debt holders always expect to get paid at the front of the line. In GM's case, the union and the government are taking 90%. The bondholders are livid. At Chrysler, the debt holders were threatened with a deal that stuffed them so badly they are still holding out against it.

The essential point I want to argue from all of this is the difference between how debt holders are being treated in the corporate world and how they are being treated in the financial world. Hold debt in a corporate, and apparently the government plays hard and crams the debts down, making the bond investors lose their money. But if those same men had bought bank debt, they would be sitting pretty with the full faith and credit of the US Treasury guaranteeing their payment.

Does this start to explain why the banks sound so confident that they will be able to raise the money they need? Does it also help us understand why bank stocks aren't dying? The US government is, in effect, herding the bond money out of dying corporations and into the ironically 'safer' financial sector. Safer, of course, only because the government is going to bail it out no matter what the cost. Why do this?

Well, if you are convinced that the bedrock of any recovery depends on first saving the banks, and if you believe that it is *only* once the banks are saved that you can set about restructuring the industrial sector, then this is the plan for you. That is why what I believe we are seeing is an engineered decoupling of the financial economy from the non-financial. In the long run it's unsustainable, but in the shorter-term the rich will have time to siphon off yet more of our wealth

I don't like it, but I feel I am starting to understand it.

8 May 09

Now it starts getting scary. A report in today's Financial Times said that further write-downs in the financial sector were due to 'a deterioration in the outlook for monoline insurers.'

That innocent little phrase should start alarm bells ringing. The monolines, such as Ambac, are insurers who insure the bond market against default. They are called monoline because they do only this one kind of insurance.

'A deterioration in outlook' is code for 'one or more of the big boys aren't going to make it.' Why not? Well, apart from the fact that bonds on corporates are defaulting, the new strain causing the hurt that gets my vote is US municipal bonds.

The monolines did a big trade in insuring the bonds issued by US towns, cities and states. All of them are now hurting like hell. The amount of aid the Federal government is having to give the states to keep them from immediate bankruptcy is at an historic high.

People have been worried about the effect of a monoline failure since the beginning of this fiasco. Maybe the municipal bond meltdown is what will finally pull one down.

9 May 09

There are more clear signs that the jaws of the vice are tightening. Costs of government borrowing are starting to go up. In the US the 30-year auction was poorly subscribed, and the rate jumped from 4.18 yield before the auction to 4.288%. Don't be fooled by how small the numbers are. A tiny move on a trillion of debt is BIG BUCKS, even for the US Treasury.

It's happening here too. In the UK the cost of borrowing is now higher than it was before the 'fix-all' quantitative easing. A measure of how spooked they are is that they have just printed and spilled another £50bn into the system. They are hoping this will bring the costs back down. But QE is like heroin: each time you need a bigger hit to get the same high.

It's not just the cost of borrowing that's causing the trouble. The other big problem governments are having is the collapse in tax revenue as the economy slows down. If you want to see the future, take a look at California: 48% collapse in tax revenue! Once the tax revenue starts to decline, it quickly becomes a downward spiral.

Increased borrowing costs, on the one hand, and decreased tax intake, on the other, mean government finances are squeezed too fast for normal levels of growth to rescue the situation. That's why I believe the authorities are trying to blow a bubble, a really huge bubble, to replace the one that burst. They hope that if they throw enough liquidity (public money to you and me) at the banks then this will inflate another speculative bubble in stocks and property.

This would, it is hoped, reinflate the value of the debt-backed paper assets and stop many losses from being realised. Then, and only then, when the bubble has refloated all the debts, would they withdraw the massive liquidity before hyperinflation takes hold. That is the bubble plan.

The risks of this plan are that the rate we have to pay on the debts to finance this may ramp up to such unsustainable levels that they could easily bankrupt the country. And that's if it works!

If it doesn't work, and I think there is a good chance it won't, then we will have a catastrophic clearing of the debts as one or more of the big banks fail. We would then have a bond market dislocation or a sovereign default. This would be followed, last but not least, by massive social unrest ending in debt repudiation.

How else will the populace react when the government tells us that things didn't go according to plan and that the money we gave to the banks has gone and is not coming back? When that happens, which it will, how are they going to spin away the unpleasant connection between bailing out a failed banking system and having to make savage cuts to the NHS? Don't they think that people will start to wake up to the fact that the death of public services is a direct consequence of the policy of bailing out the banks?

You know that classic scene in every adventure film where one of the heroes falls from a cliff/building/helicopter and is caught, rather unbelievably, by their friend? The next shot is of their hands grasping each other. They look into each other's eyes and one cries out, 'Don't you let go!', and then the happy ending ensues.

It seems to me that we are in a variation of that scene.

In our version of the scene the financial system fell over the cliff edge. The hand that went out to catch it was ours. Hanging on to it is a big fat bastard in a smart suit saying, 'Don't worry, everything is fine. I've stopped falling! A bit more help and I'll be up.'

You know what? Our version doesn't have a happy ending. The fat guy who's greasy palm you're holding is going down... Let go before he pulls you down with him.

CHAPTER 8

Debt Junkies

12 May 09

Capitalism, according to one newspaper this morning, has made a 'deathbed recovery' and, while not quite fighting fit, 'is doing well in the recovery ward.'

I beg to differ. I don't think things have fundamentally changed at all. I think all we have done is stabilise sentiment about losses. We haven't stabilized the losses themselves.

Just take losses at our old friend Freddie Mac, as one example. They were $9.9bn for the first quarter of this year. There are two very different ways we can interpret this.

First, the 'green shoots' way. This sees the loss as far smaller than the $23.9bn lost in the previous quarter, and therefore a clear sign that things are getting better.

We can also look at things a very different way. Take the year on year comparison. In the first quarter of '08, the loss was only $151 million. Now take a look at the first quarter figures for '09: a loss of $9.9 BILLION. That's a year on year increase of 6500%.

We are being sold the 'green shoots' way. The market makers have decided that irrational 'animal spirits' need to be manipulated out of fear and back into confidence. I think they have successfully frightened the short traders and flushed others into the market fearing that they might be missing the bottom. But this is very fragile. Lets look at some fundamentals. That might bring some fear back.

Just take the number of states and municipalities in the US approaching bankruptcy. The situation is very near critical. This in turn has brought the big monoline insurers into the limelight. These are the companies that insure municipal and state bonds. They are practically insolvent already. If they have to make any large payouts, this will almost certainly kill them off. Then the whole house of cards really would come tumbling down. That's one very good reason for a lot of investors to be to be afraid. Here's another.

In the US there are some accountancy law changes being proposed which, if they became law, would do something quite unthinkable: they would require the banks and other financial institutions to bring on to their books a great deal of what is currently hidden away, quite legally, off their balance sheets.

The banks, and a lot of other financial institutions, have what are known as Structured Investment Vehicles (SIVs). These are special companies set up by the banks where it is generally acknowledged they are hiding their worst losses and most toxic loans and so-called assets. To give you a brief idea of the scale of this, JP Morgan Chase has 522 SIVs; Wells Fargo has 1,181; Citigroup has 2,230; Bank of America has 2,335, and no one even knows how many Deustche Bank has.

How many more losses are hidden in these SIVs? Who knows? But you certainly don't go to so much fuss just to pass the time. If the banks had to bring these losses on to their balance sheets, then this would blow a huge gaping hole in their accounts that could only be filled by more taxpayers' money. How much more? Who knows? I don't. But what all this says to me is that those who talk about a 'deathbed recovery' are being fooled.

Of course the banks and economy have been stimulated – think of the huge amounts of cash that have been used – but they have only been revived in the way that a massive jolt of 300 volts can stimulate a corpse. If you think bringing one heart attack victim back to groggy half-life is cause to celebrate then go ahead, but please excuse me if I don't join you.

13 May 09

A very ugly truth just came out this afternoon. One that reveals how this bailout has been working in reality and who it is designed to benefit and at whose expense.

When the crisis broke AIG owed billions on credit default swaps and insurance payouts to most of the major banks, but they didn't have the money to pay. If the company hadn't been bailed out by the US taxpayer, it would have brought most of the big banks down with it.

Speaking to US lawmakers today on Capital Hill, Edward Liddy, the chief executive of AIG, said something about the nature of that bailout which proves what many of us have been saying must have been the case but until now have had no evidence to prove.

As part of the plan to save the insurance giant, the Fed set up a special financial vehicle with AIG called Maiden Lane. The Fed said that Maiden Lane would settle all those credit default swaps held by the banks that had become toxic. Just a couple of hours ago Mr Liddy said, and I quote:'The Federal Reserve decided we should pay 100 cents on the dollar.'

Sounds innocent enough. Except that he went on to admit that the Fed could have bought the same contracts for far less on the open market at the time. What does that mean? It means, clearly and unequivocally, that the Fed knowingly used taxpayers' money to overpay the banks.

Who were the banks? Goldman Sachs got $12.9bn, Société Générale got $11.9bn, Deutsche Bank got $11.8bn, and Barclays got $8.5bn. AIG was effectively used to give these ailing entities a kickback so that they could then show a profit, and the politicians could, in turn, say the 'green shoots are showing.' This is how the bailouts work. You give; they take. Their friends then cover it all up. Is this democracy? Is it even legal?

It seems to me that even the law has now been subordinated to financial expediency. Simply put, there is no longer one law for all. Any law can, it seems, be set aside to protect those who have sufficient power to demand it.

One of the oldest clichés is that the first casualty of war is always the truth, but in this case the cliché happens to be true. The financial class know, and have known all along, that they are in a war for their own survival. That is why they and their political allies regard themselves as free to lie, cheat, misinform and withhold any facts which would be inconvenient to them. That is why we would be fools to believe them.

All this, and everything else that has gone on, has really made me wonder if we need to reconsider the power relationship between democracy and finance? Has there effectively been a putsch?

I'm not the only who thinks like that. Even one of the former chief economists at the IMF, Simon Johnson, agrees. In an article in this month's issue of the Atlantic magazine entitled The Quiet Coup, Mr Johnson writes:

'The crash has laid bare many unpleasant truths about the United States. One of the most alarming is that the finance industry has effectively captured our government—a state of affairs that more typically describes emerging markets and is at the centre of many emerging-market crises. If the IMF's staff could speak freely about the US, it would tell us what it tells all countries in this situation: recovery will fail unless we break the financial oligarchy that is blocking essential reform.'

Such a situation is entirely corrosive to the rule of law, and to democracy itself, but it is, I believe, the situation we are already in. Democracy was hard to win, but it is very easy to have it taken away. And it hasn't been taken from us by foreign powers or rabid terrorists, but given away by political leaders too feeble to resist the influence and lure of the wealthy.

14 May 09

With the British election probably around a year away, some of those predicting a recovery in the economy are also suggesting that Labour might see a rise in their fortunes.

Whistle and wind are the first words that spring to my mind. It's not going to be the recovery that decides the election because there isn't going to be a recovery. What will decide it is when people start to realize the scale of the cuts necessary to repay the debt. At the moment, people have almost no sense of what is coming. When it finally hits them, everything else will pale into insignificance. If major cuts can be kicked down the road until after the election then voting will take place in relatively normal circumstances. If the scale of the pain hits people before then, all bets are off.

The brutal fact is that the cuts will be made no matter who is in power. The government, of whatever colour, will have little or no say in the matter. That is the reality we need to wake up to. This isn't a democratic question any more. Parliament and democracy ceased to have ultimate control over this country as soon as it took on an unsustainable debt. At that point, those we owe got the final say in how much we spend and what we spend it on. They are the ones who will set the levels for public spending because if they don't like what the government says then they will simply stop buying our debt.

We cannot vote this pain away. The debt has to be paid, and paid at a rate the lender dictates. Either that, or we repudiate the debt with everything that entails. That's the real horror of what we've allowed to happen.

15 May 09

The 'green shoots' cheerleaders got a bit of a shock today when it was announced that the euro zone had plunged deeper into recession with German exports and investment collapsing and France officially recorded as suffering its longest downturn since the Second World War.

That big contraction, particularly in Germany, will mean renewed pressures on their financial system as more loans go bad and others can't get rolled over. I suggest watching the German property company Hypo Real Estate for a new wobble, just like I'm watching AIG to see what new cracks appear as the weight of US commercial real estate defaults begins to bear down.

21 May 09

If things aren't looking great in Europe, they certainly aren't looking too rosy in Britain either. Standard & Poor's, the rating agency, has just downgraded their assessment of the British economy in the face of our mushrooming national debt. They described the outlook for the economy as 'negative'. They also said there was a 'one-in-three' chance that Britain would lose its AAA credit rating on its sovereign debt. If this were to happen, it would mean an even bigger increase in the cost of borrowing.

And there's the government's dilemma. On one side, there is the pressure to keep the AAA rating, meaning repayments must be faster and public spending cuts far more brutal. On the other, the banks will inevitably face greater losses and will inevitably come back for further large injections of bailout cash, cash that we don't have.

The chancellor's response to all this? To tell us it will all be over by Christmas. Weren't we told that once before?

The case of Japan should act as a warning. In the 1990s Japan had an epic property bubble. It burst. Most of its banks were swamped by a tsunami of bad debts. The government had a moment to make a clear choice. The Japanese banks thundered, as ours have done, that they could not be allowed to collapse. If they did, the government was told, Japan would be crippled, industry would shrivel and die and ordinary people would be impoverished. The government stepped in and poured trillion upon trillion of yen into its banks.

They believed, as our experts do now, that the policy would reinflate the economy. Pumping money into the banks would increase lending, people would spend, industry would produce, and the new wealth would pour back into the banks who would repay their debt. That was the theory. In reality what it gave them was ten years of zero growth: 'the lost decade'. Now Japanese exports have fallen off another cliff and so has their GDP. A lost two decades! We are, almost precisely, following their footsteps.

Our entire government strategy, both here and in the US, is based on a single fundamental article of faith that the Japanese shared. That article of faith states that the crisis is one of liquidity not solvency. It is based on the belief that the banks have otherwise valuable assets that have just temporarily lost their real value. Brown, Darling, Obama and the rest have all bet the house, at least yours and mine, on this being true.

I think they are wrong. Liquidity is not the cause, but a symptom of the fact that the banks' underlying assets are in fact worthless. I think the losses will continue to blister and suppurate. I think more bailouts will be forced upon us. We will see higher borrowing, more printing and the costs of all borrowing creeping up and up until it is unsustainable.

People may think I'm being alarmist, but in the end it doesn't matter what I think: it's what the rating agencies think that counts. It doesn't even matter that some people think the rating agencies are fools or crooks. If the investors, the potential buyers of our debt, take notice then the rating agencies' opinions, right or wrong, have a critical effect. And what they are seeing are reasons to be concerned that we may soon have to borrow or print a great deal more.

It is under this unpleasant picture that we will see the reality of public pensions being gutted, private pensions funds failing, unemployment rising and savage cuts in welfare spending.

Is that alarmist? I certainly hope so!

28 May 09

Now here's a sign of things to come. China's Beijing Automotive Industry Corp has just withdrawn from talks to buy General Motors Europe. That is really significant. Do you think that signals Chinese confidence in a recovery for European made motors?

Keep abreast of what China is doing. The Chinese have more cash than Midas at the moment. They could have bought

GM Europe if they wanted to. So why didn't they? Could it be that in the end they thought they would be better doing what GM America has already talked to them about: making the cars in China and exporting them to us? That way they keep the investment and skilled work in China.

And it's not just the motor industry where China is worth watching. One of the most interesting developments has been their buying of land in Africa. They have been buying lots of it. Why do you suppose that is? Food shortages anyone? Imperialism without armies. You don't invade: you just buy it. All perfectly legal. And as long as you can buy the government as well, you can do what you like.

Finally, China has been on a long, eight months and more, buying spree for all raw materials. They have also been buying gold and gold mines at an amazing rate. China is now the largest producer of gold. What's more, the Chinese government has been encouraging their citizens to buy gold. What this suggests is that the Chinese are trying to offset their holdings of dollar debt by also having gold and other minerals. Could this be the standard for a new reserve currency based on raw materials? I think it could.

That's what they have been buying. What about what they have been selling? Well, as we know, they have been selling as much long-dated US government debt as they can without spooking the market. Instead they have been buying short-dated debt. This means they can get out of their US dollar debt more quickly.

Put all this together, and I think this tells us that the largest debt buyer in the world is clearly saying it has no confidence of a recovery in US real estate or US manufacturing. In addition, it tells us the Chinese are increasingly nervous about the dollar and the debt it backs. The Chinese actions (not their words) tell us that the Chinese are pricing in a growing chance of dollar devaluation or default. Both unthinkable, I know. But you never think you will get run over by a bus until it happens.

It says to me the Chinese are preparing a plan B. We don't have such a plan.

4 June 09

Someone asked me earlier today if I really thought we in the West would see no recovery at all. Well, I can see the possibility of some recovery, but it's two-tier, and it's not very good news for most of us.

Once upon a time, the FTSE and the Dow Jones were seen as accurate proxies for the overall health of the broader economy, but maybe not any longer. I have raised this possibility before, but I think we might have soon given the financial system so much money, bailed them out so successfully, that we will see them finally decouple from the rest of the economy. In these circumstances, we could quite easily see a 'recovery' in the financial system but a worsening of the situation in the real economy.

With the money we have given the banks, they could feasibly be able to trade sustainably amongst themselves. This would fuel a stock market bubble in certain sectors favoured by the speculators. At the same time, firms in the real economy would be going bankrupt and unemployment would be growing.

At first we will be told that these discrepancies with the real economy are just lagging indicators, but slowly it will be come apparent that these are not lagging: they are simply not connected at all. What we will have is a paper recovery in the financial sector; what we won't have is a recovery made from either consumption or manufacturing.

Every rise you see in the markets will simply be a measure of how well the financial class is doing. And the reason they will be doing well is because they have left the rest of us behind to pay off their old debts, like the debt slaves we will have become.

19 June 09

More warnings came today from commentators nervous that the 'recovery' in the real economy is going to be slower than they thought. These gentleman really need to get out a bit more.

Let's just look at one hard fact before believing that there will be any sort of recovery at all in any quarter of this year, or of next. Next week alone, the US government has to sell $165bn in treasuries. If it has to sell the same amount each week, that is an annual rate of $5.58 TRILLION! But worse than the astounding scale of the debt is the short duration of the bonds: instead of being safely tied away in 10 or 30-year bonds, $101bn of this debt is for between two years to only six-months.

That means the debt will be back on the market in two years or less and will have to be refinanced along with any new debt that is needed. This is unsustainable. You cannot roll over that much debt that often. It creates massive volatility and equally massive political instability. One hiccup in the market and... BOOM.

The bond market will then have governments over a barrel in a way we have never seen. They will demand higher and higher rates on our debt until we cut our deficits. Rates are already going up. This in turn has pushed up US mortgage rates, killing house sales and putting an end to hopes that a new US housing bubble will solve all our problems. The same grim picture looks likely to unfold here as well.

These are solid factual reasons you should not believe in speculation that recovery is a mere quarter away. If anything we are getting closer to a double dip.

24 June 09

This is interesting. It looks like the rats running the ship might be starting to fight amongst themselves. Speaking this afternoon in front of a treasury select committee, Mervyn King attacked the chancellor's borrowing plans and suggested that without 'decisive action' (i.e. massive spending cuts), the government would have great difficulty funding its deficit in the coming years.

What King is saying is a reflection of what the bond market is telling him. That's the bottom line, not party political allegiance. He is passing on the message, in guarded central banker speak, that the bond market will NOT continue to buy our debt, at all, if we don't make savage cuts in public spending to take almost immediate effect. When he says, 'in the course of a single parliament', he could not ring the alarm bell any more loudly! He means NOW.

King, as governor of the Bank of England, gets no power or gain from meddling in politics. Quite the opposite: he risks personal damage and professional harm. So the fact that he is sticking his little pointy-head so far up into the firing line means we should listen carefully.

King knows the banks are facing another round of very large losses. He knows house price declines in the US and here are putting even prime mortgages underwater and into default – the same with commercial real estate.

He is also reading better sources than I have, and I think they're telling him China is not going to save world trade but is turning inwards to feed a domestic market. He is also very aware that China has a pending real estate crash of its

own which it will have to deal with if it doesn't want to see
its own banks crippled.

You don't have to like King, but you would be a fool not to
listen to the message he is conveying. He is the messenger.
It's the message you want to pay attention to.

There never were any fundamental improvements on which
to base a recovery. All the fundamentals point down. But if
you throw over £500bn and over a trillion dollars at any
problem, you can make it levitate for a while. That's all.

All the money was never going to do anything but buy time
in which it was hoped 'confidence' would inflate things
again. The problem is it hasn't. The tragedy is that we have
now taken on so much debt that getting out from under it
will be much more traumatic than if we had faced the debts
to start with.

I have no idea what idiotic actions our governments will take,
but I'd be willing to bet they will not address the underlying
problem of uncleared debts and hidden losses. They will
react, as they have done all along, with policies designed to
continue to hide the debts and protect the financial class from
suffering the losses they have made. A prolonging of such
idiot policies will only deepen and extend the catastrophe.

10 July 09

I believe we are starting to get signs of another round of
banking pain coming up.

Look at CIT. This is the bank that used to be called
Commercial Credit and Investment Company. Two years ago,
they were a lender to 950,000 businesses and were trading
at $59 a share. Yesterday, those shares fell to $1.56 and their
bonds were trading as junk. They can hang on for a while,
but unless they get a major bailout they are toast.

Why tell you this mindless detail? Because the truth is in the detail, not in the self-serving, rose-tinted operation 'restore confidence' burblings of our politicians.

Take a look at AIG if you are in any doubt. It has already been bailed out three times to the tune of $185bn and is still sinking. In just seven days its share price went from $30 to $10. The hundred billion dollar stake the US taxpayer bought will be worth nothing according to AIG itself. Their chief executive has just admitted that more losses are coming up with little chance of the US government ever being able to give up its majority ownership. Bear this in mind when 'experts' tell you how we are buying valuable assets which we will make money on in the end.

Green shoot cheerleaders should also pay some attention to what is happening with prime mortgages in the US. Defaults on these mortgages are now 6% and rising. This really matters because these mortgages are what make up the 'best' senior tranches of the mortgage-backed securities. The banks are still holding them at close to face value and haven't written them down. When they do, they are going to show up as new losses demanding fresh bailouts.

But it isn't just mortgages. Rising unemployment means rising defaults on credit card loans into the bargain. These have rocketed up from 6-7% to 9% and more. The biggest losses are at Citigroup and AmEx. As I have said before, I don't think Citigroup will make it.

As for the rally in stocks, see it for what it is: 60-70% of the volume on Wall Street every day is machine driven trades from a handful of big houses. This means that there is little real buyer sentiment. A few traders are trading stocks back and forth driving up the price. The price rise does not reflect any underlying improvement in the companies or the economy. It is purely an artifact of machine trading. The day they stop trading, the price will crash vertically. Small traders who have been sucked in to chase the 'rally' will be left holding the loss.

And one more thing worth remembering. Most of these large traders are trading with Fed money given to them in the bailout. It appears to me that the financial sector has learnt nothing and does not intend to change one iota. They have taken us for every penny we had and will take our children for every penny they have.

6 Aug 09

Yet more evidence that the financial system is gradually decoupling from the rest of the economy. The banks announced big losses yesterday, and yet their shares rose. Wide-eyed pundits say this is because 'they know the worst is now over.' Believe at your peril. They rallied because they knew the government would bail them out, again. And sure enough today they did: quantitative easing to the rescue. The Bank of England is pumping another £50bn into the banks. This brings the total already through QE to £175bn. Over a third more! Does that tell you something? It should. £125bn, more than the whole annual budget for the National Health Service, HAS NOT WORKED! The sickness continues. This is not the end.

Will all this help the rest of the economy? Absolutely not! And if I hear another City apologist say it does, I will puke. Any way you cut it, QE is to funnel money to the banks. Barely a brass farthing will make it to us. Every time there is talk of more QE is because the central bank needs to get yet more of our wealth into the banks without having to admit to another bailout

Has QE increased lending to business? No, not so far. Does QE help the unemployed? No, how would it?

Does it ease unemployment levels? No, not when there is no lending to business.

Does it magically help retail sales? No, not when people are frightened of losing their jobs.

So what does QE do? What is it really for? Remember, worldwide, we are talking about several trillions of dollars, euros and pounds. It hasn't flowed into private or corporate lending. It isn't flowing into commercial real estate. So where has so much money gone? Direct to the banks of course.

A significant part of the newly printed money is being used to buy back UK gilts from the banks and other financial institutions in the hope that this new cash will be used to stimulate lending to the rest of the economy. The problem is the banks haven't increased their lending. The credit markets are still virtually shut.

The government have said this is because the effects of QE take time to filter through. This is, at best, a half-truth. If the QE money had been used by the banks to stimulate lending, it would have come through a while ago. It hasn't. We have had a year or more of mewling, impotent half-wits from government and opposition alike complaining about it.

What these simpletons don't seem to realise is that they have given our money to the wrong people. In order for real growth and sustainable recovery to happen we all need investment by investors. People who take money and invest it in some sort of wealth production. Investment creates jobs, which creates income, which creates spending and demand, which then leads to producers needing more investment to produce more goods to meet more demand. Let's leave aside the fundamental injustices of capitalism and the practicalities of endless growth in a finite world – just for today – and bask in the warmth of this idealized world.

The fact today, which our politicians fail to understand, is that our financial markets no longer invest in order to primarily help production. That sort of investment is old-fashioned because growth from investment in machines and people takes time. If you invest in production, in machines and people, you need to wait to recoup that investment. You also need stability.

Investment today, as far as the banks are concerned, is all about speculation. To speculate you don't need any real world stuff at all. It's about betting on derivatives and credit default swaps and other unworldly stuff for rewards that are instantaneous.

And this, as I see it, is the nightmare we are in. Our central bankers gave out our money hoping for investment in jobs, in people and all those other trite political phrases. But they forgot one thing: the people they gave our money to were speculators, not investors. They were the raddled and ruined high-rolling debt junkies, choking and coughing up their own putrid debts, whose addiction to risk and reward had led to the crisis in the first place.

So what has happened? Well, some of the money has gone to shore up the holes in the banks' balance sheets left by their rotting assets. The rest has gone into speculation on stocks, on currency trades and betting on sovereign defaults because that is the only growth that will save them. It's high risk, but it has high rewards, and they need that instantaneous rush of risk and debt – the speedball addiction – to stave off the implosion of their asset values. Their veins are rotten, their bodies addled, but, like all junkies, they always need just one more fix.

And these are the people our politicians have given all our money to: addicts hooked on debt. They don't produce anything. They don't do anything of social use or value. All they do is gamble with debt. And these are the very people our politicians look to for salvation?

But it gets worse. The more *we* become steeped in debt – due to bailing them out – the more *we* must have the instantaneous growth that only speculation can give. They are leading us down the same path. Only by getting us to buy the same crap that ruined them can they pay for that big fix they all believe will return them to debt junkie heaven.

So what now for us? Are we going to do as we are told when they tell us that another stimulus is what we need? More debt? More cuts to pay for it? Are we going to carry on feeding their habit? Are *we* hooked as well? Wake up please.

14 Aug 09

While the big banking boys are in their City den mainlining on the latest dose of QE, their little wannabe debt junkie politician friends are behind the bike sheds getting high on the latest rise in UK house prices.

Some people just never learn. This fixation on UK house prices as a key indicator of the economy is at best myopic and parochial, at worst plain ignorant.

Just as the economic crisis was not triggered here but in the US, so its continuation is not dependent on conditions here but on those in the US. All the lending markets between banks, the stock markets around the globe and the bond markets depend on what happens to the US economy, so let's look at what is happening there.

Commercial real estate is the big wave that some of us, including me, thought would have broken by now. This sector has been in crisis for six months or so, but as yet none of the banks' assets based on commercial real estate have been valued at anything near their actual sale value. The banks have preferred to roll over, or simply not recognise, the losses on these commercial loans. Basically a hide and pretend accounting strategy.

They can do that so long as our governments continue to give them bailout cash to plug the capital and assets crater left by these defaulting loans. As the commercial real estate sector goes deeper into crisis, this will make bigger and bigger holes in the banks' balance sheets.

Just yesterday, Alabama's second largest bank was declared bankrupt. The losses at this one bank are larger than the entire bank rescue fund of the Federal Deposit Insurance Scheme (FDIC). So the FDIC will now have to go to the US Treasury to get more money. The Treasury will have to print or borrow that money.

After this, there are 150 more publicly traded banks in the US all of which have non-performing loans equal to or more than 5% of their holdings. That percentage, with typical bank leverage, is more than enough to make them bankrupt as well. Together these 150 banks on the dead and dying list have $193bn in deposits. Will they go bust? Without our help to feed their habit, almost certainly!

28 Aug 09

The real truth about UK house price rises is now becoming clear. It seems the bankers might have laced the little taster they gave our politicians with something quite nasty.

I think the clue to understanding the truth about the house prices rises is to see that they occurred in Wales and north-east England. Think about that for just a second. Wales and north-east England at the forefront of a finance driven recovery? How likely does that seem?

The answer is not complicated. The banks have been selling the properties they have repossessed to themselves. Or rather to off-balance sheet subsidiaries of their own creation, which buy the properties at the banks' full asking price. RBS set up a company called West Register to do this. Other banks have done the same. US banks are doing something similar over there. First they hid the bad loans. Now it seems they are trying to hide the properties as well.

It's quite a trick. Suddenly houses are being sold, so there are good sales figures to report. At the same time, prices are kept high, so there are good price figures to report. The banks claim their subsidiary 'pays what the property would fetch on the open market'. Not forgetting to add the important proviso that this price has to be 'fair value'.

'Fair value' is one of those phrases much loved by financiers. Who decides fair value? You guessed it: they do. It's their old friend mark-to-model. First you make noises about 'impaired assets' and 'dysfunctional markets'. By dint of those magic phrases you dismiss the actual prices in the real market, and in their place you work out for yourself the 'fair value'.

This is the same 'fair value' being worked out between the Treasury and the banks for the value of the assets they are putting into the government's insurance scheme.

If, as they claim, the subsidiary pays what the property would fetch on the open market then why not sell it on the open market? You don't have to be Einstein or some conspiracy theorist to realise how this works. Some people might think this is illegal, but they would be wrong. It is all perfectly legal, proper and above board. That is how the system works.

We give them money so that they can maintain house prices at a higher level than if they were sold on the open market. At the same time, they can show the money they are 'lending' to their off-balance sheet companies buying the properties as proof that they are 'lending' to the wider economy. Finally, if in a year or two's time they find they own and can't sell lots of properties – for which they probably massively overpaid – they can come back to us for another bailout. No doubt telling us we need to cut government services and spending to pay for it.

It just shows you should never underestimate the cunning of someone who needs to feed a habit.

29 Aug 09

It seems it is not only house prices where there are strange things going on. Last week more that 30% of the entire New York Stock Exchange trade volume was in just five financial stocks: Citigroup, AIG, CIT, Fannie and Freddie. They all saw increases in trade volume of several hundred percent.

All these companies are in debt to the US government to the tune of billions None of them could survive without that money. Just yesterday, a pretty well-informed analyst made it clear that Fannie and Freddie are so utterly ruined by bad debts that they will *never* return to profitability. And yet billions of shares were traded and up, up, up went their stocks. It would seem to me that someone is manipulating the market on a scale no one has ever seen.

One theory doing the rounds is that the US government is pumping money into these firms through the back-door by giving others money and telling them to buy stocks in the companies the government wants to help. Who knows? I don't. What I do know is that five insolvent financial companies have seen their shares shoot up to completely dominate the entire New York Stock Exchange and in so doing ramp up the entire exchange. Five insolvent financial firms owning the world's largest slices of global bad debt are the reason for the 'recovery' on the NYSE?

A good sign? I don't think so.

30 Aug 09

Ooooh. Seems like some of our politicians might have already been getting into the hard stuff, possibly weapons-grade. If they have, things could get very nasty.

I have been looking at levels of debt being issued by the US, UK, Euroland and others, and while I don't have accurate figures – they're hard to come by – I think there is no longer enough actual cash around to support all the debt being issued.

In 'normal' times China and Japan would, for example, buy US debt with foreign currency from exports. Because they both have a trade surplus with the US they have lots of dollars that they need to return, so they buy US treasuries. The US gets its dollars back, and the buyer gets 'safe' US treasuries to hold. The problem today is that exports have crashed, so that source of foreign currency has dried up. Foreign reserves aren't flush either. So what 'money' is being used to 'buy' the debt? Because the fact is that it is still being sold in stupendous amounts.

I think there is now the distinct possibility that central banks may be using QE, or even their own debt, to buy other people's debt. If I am correct, then the debt market has become like one of those Escher drawings where the stairs seem to go up and up impossibly. I hope I am wrong because if not, the nightmare is only just beginning. Nation states would be engaging in the same insane round of bubble finance that destroyed the banks.

This is how it works. You lend me £10, and in exchange I give you an IOU for that amount. A few minutes later, I lend you the same £10 you just gave me, and *you* now give *me* an IOU in return. No one has any more actual money, but we are now *both* holding IOUs for £10. Because we are very clever/stupid/desperate (take your pick) we decide to count these IOUs as AAA 'money good' and file them on our own balance sheets as Full Value Capital Asset. Despite there being no more real money, we now both have lots more money in our accounts. Magic! Party on guys! Now imagine doing that with billions and billions of dollars. That's exactly what the banks did in the years before the crisis. That's part of how they all got hooked on debt. It is quite a high while it lasts, as you can imagine.

I am rather worried that in their desperation to finance the bank bailouts and stimulus plans our governments are now repeating this madness on an even larger scale. If this is what our governments are doing, they are fuelling a massive sovereign debt bubble. If I am in any way correct then this is folly in the extreme. Who will bail out nation states when this sovereign debt bubble bursts and governments find *they* are left holding worthless bits of paper? No one can. GAME OVER.

10 Sept 09

I find it more difficult to write these days because so many people seem to buying the, 'It's all over, and the worst is behind us' line.

The problem is I cannot convince myself that what I am being assured is correct. I cannot help but see that what they say is best for us all is, in fact, only best for the financial class and their attendant pimps, priests and soothsayers.

Let's all watch the stock market rise, and not ask who for? Let's all cheer as borrowing costs and the costs of insuring the debts go down, but not ask whose debt, and incurred for what end and whose benefit? Let's all feel relieved that a meltdown was averted and not ask how the 'solution' will be paid for? Let's all watch the bankers feast and not ask about what happens when the waiter brings *us* the bill?

Maybe it's best not to ask any of these questions. Let's just listen to the voices telling us that happiness depends on the banks doing well and the consumer spending again. Let's slip numbly into the role allotted to us: happy bovine consumers.

Do you suppose cattle feel better not thinking ahead? Do you think they save themselves pointless fretting and lead happier lives by filling their minds with gratitude and warm feeling for the man who brings them hay and leads them to a place to sleep each night? I think they probably *are* happier knowing their future is being looked after by someone who cares for them and is, after all, so much cleverer than they are.

So I'm sorry for not being a happy cow. I just don't see it that way.

To me it seems that what is happening now has very clear and disturbing echoes of what happened in the thirties.

In late 1929, after the earlier crash, the stock markets here and in the States rallied *more* than they have over the last few months. Then, as now, there were powerful and 'expert' market watchers who proclaimed, 'It's over' and broke out the champagne. On November 14, 1929, Irving Fisher, the most famous and revered economist of his time, assured the world that the decline in markets would be over 'in a few more days at most.' Just weeks later, the market failed and fell like a rock to depths no one was prepared for. The real Depression was only just beginning.

When stocks were rallying there was no improvement in unemployment, none in manufacturing, and none in forward-looking profit. And it was these things that eventually squeezed the life out of the make-believe of stock speculation 'recovery'.

The stocks are rallying now because of all the hundreds of billions pumped in to give an absolute guarantee to certain sectors of the economy that they will not be allowed to lose. With such a guarantee, and all that bailout money, why wouldn't those stocks rally?

So when you hear that the recession is over, remember to ask whose recession? The bankers have been given a gold-plated, get-out-of-debt-free card. For the rest of us, the recession is here for many, many years.

Their debts have been shovelled relentlessly on to the public purse. Our debt is now correspondingly massive. Those massive losses are now straining our national credit rating as our borrowing rockets out of control. And, what do you know? The voices that urged the taking on of the debt to fund the bailouts are now the same voices telling us the dire consequences of having the debt and how we must cut spending to bring it down.

Suddenly, 'caution', 'prudence' and 'belt-tightening' are going to be the only words we hear. Isn't it funny how no such worries occurred to any of the decision makers when it was the banks that needed money? It is only *after* all the debt been piled on to us, and the proceeds given to the banks, that the cost of debt becomes an issue.

Now, when it comes to unemployment, poverty, homelessness, children going to overcrowded and rundown schools, suddenly the talk is of debt being unsustainable. Never a hint of less borrowing when any bank needs it. Only cuts to compensate afterwards. That was always the plan. Save them, at our cost. Now that the financial aristocracy have been protected is when we get to listen to our leaders telling us how 'we' can't afford to help people who aren't 'systemically important'. That's us, 'not systemically important'. We're just the expendable foot soldiers for the debt junkie lords.

CHAPTER 9

The Maginot Line

14 Oct 09

I have needed some time to reconsider my thoughts. I think I have been wrong about the crisis.

I have been wrong, over the last year or so, when I have said that bailing out the banks wouldn't work. I was wrong because I didn't think you could suspend the law of gravity. Events have proved otherwise. Apparently, if you have $1.5 trillion or so to spend, you can. I stand humbled and corrected.

If a friend of yours falls off a cliff carrying a boulder of debt the size of your car, you can keep him, and his debt, suspended in mid-air having a champagne party. All you have to do is rob the country of vast sums of money and throw it at the problem. Of course, if you stop paying – SPLAT! Gravity resumes.

And that's the problem. It's not a one-off payment. We have to keep spending this sort of money. The banks have a lot more loans going bad in prime, jumbo and commercial loan books. They are bleeding badly. And, don't forget, they don't just hold loans: they hold securities based on loans, derivatives based on those, and credit default swaps guaranteeing or betting against the lot. Most of the securities are now worth far less than the banks paid, while the potential losses in credit default swaps alone are in the hundreds of billions. If all that isn't enough, there are the unknown losses the banks have hidden away, off-balance sheet, in structured investment vehicles and the like.

The banks are still so insanely leveraged they simply don't have the money to cover even relatively small losses. That's why the only thing I can see is one catastrophe after another needing one bailout after another.

Despite this, I am no longer saying we will, or must, have a second crash. I used to say that. Now I know better. What I am saying now is that we will have a second round of bank losses – some of which will be kicked further down the road, and some of which will come back to us as another round of bailouts.

At that point, the crushing effects of paying the interest on the debts we have already taken on will be immense. The bankers will be asking for money at the same time that public spending on schools, health and pensions are all being gutted. What do you think our brave politicians will do then? Will they stand up to the banks and admit that all the debt incurred so far has been for nothing? Or will they cravenly lick the spittle from the corner of the bankers' mouths as they tell us that we must give the bankers yet more money, no matter how many cuts to vital services that entails.

And what will we do then? Will we finally have the spine to stand together and give a morally corrupt political and financial class the kicking it deserves, or will we shiver fearfully in the corner and do as we are told?

22 Oct 09

An important bit of news surfaced today that sheds an interesting light on the real state of bank balance sheets.

When experts talk of 'withdrawing the stimulus', part of what they mean is taking cash out of the system. One way the Fed does this is by means of what they call a 'reverse repo'.

This involves the Fed offering to sell some securities to the banks in exchange for cash, but promising to buy them back later for a small, agreed profit to the banks. For the banks it's a sweet deal as they get to make a guaranteed profit without any risk. But what does the Fed get out of it? Well, the Fed uses it as a way of controlling the amount of liquidity in the system to prevent inflation getting out of its box. If they think there is too much liquidity, they can have a reverse repo and try to calm things down a little.

The surprise this week was that the Fed had a reverse repo auction, and no one turned up. Given that the banks could make an easy, risk-free profit, one has to ask why? I think the answer is that none of the big banks wants, or is able, to return any of the bailout cash they were given. The Fed and other central banks can't have their money back because the banks need it to plug the hole left by assets now worth much less than the banks want to reveal. Take out the money and 'puff' – there go the balance sheet lies up in smoke.

We have, as British politicians like to say, produced a double whammy. First, we can't get our money back. Second, that money isn't doing any 'stimulating' now, and it won't be doing any in the future. All it has done is provide life support for the dead and dying. Those promises of future profitability are just that – promises. A banker would laugh in your face if the tables were reversed and the promises were yours.

23 Oct 09

I think there are further signs that we are headed for another large freezing of credit markets.

The banks are clearly hoarding cash. As far as anyone can see, most of what they do have is tied up settling inter-bank debts day to day. Other cash is low. Morgan Stanley seems to have only $31bn in cash to cover $700bn in debt liability. On the face of it that is insane leverage. I am also hearing from people I trust saying that Morgan's cash position is actually getting worse not better.

This is happening at the same time the big credit card issuers, Capital One, and Citigroup, have just jacked up their rates from 21% to 31%. This is punitive. Anyone who can transfer their account to another lender will. Why would Capital One and Citigroup do this? Are they trying to reduce their exposure to credit debt? It's an extreme and very costly way of doing it, but if they think another credit freeze is coming then it makes some sense.

Something is definitely wrong.

24 Oct 09

Yesterday I wrote about the growing cash shortage at the big banks. Today the Federal Deposit Insurance Corporation (FDIC) has had to take control of its 100th regional bank, Capmark, one of the US's largest commercial real estate lenders.

The rumour is that Capmark will file for Chapter 11 bankruptcy this weekend. It will be interesting to see if they do, or if they can hold out for a little longer. If they collapse, they would be the second really large commercial real estate lender to go under. This is going to be just the beginning of a whole wave of commercial real estate carnage.

But it's not just commercial real estate. There is a general wipe-out happening across the board. The last two banks the FDIC closed were both reported to be well-capitalised right up to the day they exploded. Then, as soon as the books were opened, shock, horror! Instead of being well-capitalised the FDIC discovers the banks are sitting on 45-50% losses on assets held on the books at near 100%.

There are a lot of other banks in the same position. This is why, as the cash flow dries up, I think we will see another crisis emerging in the banking sector. These are early days yet; I could be quite wrong, but it's worth watching carefully. The future does not look good.

2 Nov 09

The cheery news keeps coming. Citigroup, now undisputed king of the walking dead, is awash with rumours of another $10bn in write-downs, most of it from mortgage-backed securities. And they won't be the last. Figures from last year show Citigroup has over a TRILLION in lending on its books and ANOTHER TRILLION in lending, which it keeps locked away *off* its books. The company is *only* worth $87bn, so just a small percentage of defaults would wipe out their whole value.

Then (not to be confused with Citigroup) there is CIT, the specialist small and medium-sized business lender. After months of vainly trying to get its bondholders to swap debt for equity, it has finally filed for Chapter 11 bankruptcy. The fact that the bondholders opted for bankruptcy is telling. It says they prefer to get back what they can of their money now rather than hope CIT can return more money later through future profits.

This is extremely significant. The bond market is saying they don't think those small and medium-sized businesses that owe CIT are going to be able to pay but are more likely to go bankrupt and default instead.

If the bond players are correct, that's not good news for the credit card companies. If small businesses can't make it, that's because their customers aren't bringing enough money through the door. The mad binge is over. Could it be the huge debt burden means the US consumer isn't spending and is defaulting on the credit they have taken out?

For a while buying stuff is what made people feel happy and secure. Do people now have the desire to spend, spend, spend at anything like the levels required to inflate our way back up the cliff? Not any longer it seems. Stuff equals debt, equals insecurity. It's a different world. That has big implications because without spending the consumption and debt model of capitalism is bust. The only people who don't seem to see this are our politicians.

For what is the great vision of salvation they offer us? It is simply to exhort us to spend, consume, throw away and consume again. Return to growth. Growth at all costs. Make more, consume more, and be happy in your debt. That is their vision. Riches today by spending what a future generation will have to pay off. Consumption now with no regard for its future consequences. Their solution, that we 'must return lending and consumption back to boom time levels', just shows how utterly intellectually and morally lost they are.

Because they are so lost, they are unable to see beyond saving the banks, whatever the cost. In many ways, bailing out the banks has become their version of the Maginot Line. The generals thought France was in danger, and the only solution their thinking allowed was to build a defensive line. The costs, no matter how ruinous, were therefore worth it. To oppose it was to be classed as either an idiot or a traitor.

In the minds of the French generals, the Maginot Line was an impregnable defence that would keep disaster at bay. As it took shape, it looked bold and impressive. Once started, it had a momentum of its own. How could one think of abandoning the project once you realized how much had been spent already? To change course, and listen to the doubters' suggestions of building modern tanks and aircraft instead, would have made a mockery of all the money spent on their wall so far. Therefore, despite all the accumulating arguments that highly mobile German armour and aircraft might just make their static defence obsolete, no expense was spared, and money was kept pouring in to build the defences.

I cannot help but look at bank bailouts and see the same catastrophic failure of the imagination at work.

People keep proclaiming that we couldn't have done things any differently. They claim the ATM system would have collapsed. They say we would have all lost our savings and that our mortgages would have been called in. None of this is true. We could have done lots of other things.

We could have allowed the insolvent banks to go down and be taken into receivership. Their businesses could have been wound down and sold off. It happens to businesses everyday. Most people would not have lost their money because it comes under the government guarantee. For a fraction of the money we have wasted so far, we could have set up several brand new debt free banks. Banks that would have lent to business, administered the ATM system and taken over mortgages.

The worrying thing for me was that not only was there never any debate, but none was allowed. Our political class has been completely captured, both intellectually and morally, by the financial class and its ruling ideology. They could only ever see one solution: a solution that meant the rich kept their wealth at the expense of everyone else.

But the trap is that their solution has a severe economic and political time limit. Economically, assets and stock markets have to regain their profitability quickly before fear takes hold and the rats start to abandon ship again. Politically, finances have to right themselves before a popular revolt sweeps governments from power as the stark reality of public impoverishment becomes clear.

Both clocks are ticking.

6 Nov 09

It seems like one clock just started going a lot more quickly. Unemployment in the US went up to 10% last month. This 10% is just the U3 figure. U6 – which includes those no longer looking and those in low-paying part-time work – is up at 17.5% or so. And the figure is accelerating, not decelerating.

These figures mean there can be absolutely no recovery in consumer spending. Businesses hoping for salvation at Christmas will get a pitiful blip, at most, followed by deepening misery afterwards. Those who listened to the 'green shoots' brigade and overstocked will be in pain.

And it's not just the retail and employment figures that are looking grim. It was only last quarter that our old friend Fannie Mae made a $19bn loss and needed bailing out. Well, now they have declared more losses and need a further $15bn bailout. What's worse is that both of these losses have come before the main wave of Alt-A and Option ARM hits.

And that's not all. If the problem with Fannie Mae were just the losses, we would be laughing. But the real problem is much nastier. The Fed has bought $1.25 trillion of Fannie and Freddie paper.

If Fannie is making more than $15bn losses every quarter then the value of the assets they sold to the Fed is going to crash. Would you want to be holding assets in a company making $15bn losses a quarter? Of course not, but the Fed is, and it has no way out. It will be left holding a huge basket of almost worthless paper. What do you think that will do for the US credit rating?

You hear that rumbling? That's the sound of Niagara Falls. Stop listening to the fools in the boat who are prattling on about how they have it all under control. *They* will get lifted to safety at the last moment. *We* will all be going over the edge.

7 Nov 09

It's not just Fannie and Freddie or the US banks that are in trouble. There was some revealing news yesterday about the assets RBS put into the government's insurance scheme.

The details in the report are thin, but it seems £51bn of the assets in the scheme are related to commercial mortgages, while another £38bn are, 'connected to monoline insurers.' Both commercial mortgages and the monolines are in massive trouble. If RBS has to swallow any of these losses, it could kill off any last desperate attempt at life support.

If people are in any doubt, just look at the numbers. RBS has already used up £27bn of the £60bn we gave it to cover losses. With more losses likely to come they will easily get through the remaining £33bn very quickly. They will then require the 'emergency' £8bn that Darling said he was setting aside for them. Once they run through that, because of our suicidal insurance scheme we are then on the hook for 90% of any more losses.

RBS are going down and will be dragging us with them. That's quite a legacy Alistair. Well done.

24 Nov 09

Even the IMF are waking up to the bank losses yet to come. Yesterday their high priest, Mr Stauss-Kahn, said he estimated that only half of bank losses have been revealed so far. That means we still have about $1.5 TRILLION in losses to come.

Do people realise how serious this is? Our national borrowing is already at crisis point, and we have only coped with the first half of losses!

Just look at the situation in the US. Congress estimates that the government will need to borrow $3.5 TRILLION more over the next few years. That is only the US, and only for the debts declared so far. And don't forget, much of the debt already issued was only bought as short-term bonds, some for only one to three month's duration. That means, in addition to the $3.5 trillion of new debt, a lot of recently sold debt has to new find buyers when it comes back onto the market again in just a few months' time.

Now let's add in the $1.5 trillion estimated undeclared bad debts on top. Have your eyes begun to water yet? I bet Ben Bernanke's have.

30 Nov 09

Today we got our first taste of some of the banking losses still to come. Ever since they started building castles in the sand Dubai has been a disaster just waiting to happen. Dubai World, the property company doing most of the building, have just announced they can't pay $59bn debts. This has sent shock waves through the City and Wall Street as many of our banks are the ones who gave out the loans – RBS being one of the biggest lenders. Well, the big shock for all them was that the Dubai government has just said they won't bail out Dubai World. Good for them, but guess who will?

Remember that asset insurance scheme Alistair Darling set up for the banks? Well RBS put many of these loans to Dubai World into it, so *we* will pay for their losses. And while RBS made the loans other banks will have bought the securities based on those loans. So even some of the banks that didn't make direct loans are going to suffer losses. They too will be back for more bailouts from their governments in the West.

This is where Mr Darling's wonderful insurance scheme has ended up. The Dubai government won't bail out Dubai World, so we will.

In my opinion the Dubai government is quite correct. The irony is that an undemocratic government have responded in a democratic and lawful way. They have made those who made the losses obey the law and suffer the consequences, while we here in the West have been revealed as a bunch of banana republics where the rich control the government and fleece the public purse as and when they please.

8 Dec 09

Ooops! All hands on deck! Emergency! Emergency! There were the bankers congratulating themselves for having come through the latest little storm when, WHOOSH, there's a sudden roaring sound, and the ship started to list very badly to one side. Turns out some Greek deckhand had left the car-deck doors open and the sea is pouring in.

Greece is now looking like she really could default. Fitch's, the rating agency, has cut Greece's long-term national debt rating from A- to BBB+. Two more notches down and it's as good as junk. This is dangerous territory, and everyone knows it. As soon as the news broke the euro dropped like a stone, and markets all over the world started selling off. They are all frightened that Greece could start a cascade of indebted nations defaulting on their loans.

In a clear state of anxiety, the head of the European Central
Bank, Jean-Claude Trichet, appealed to the Greek prime
minister, George Papandreou, to enact, 'very difficult, very
courageous but absolutely necessary measures.' By this he
doesn't mean making the rich Greeks who avoided paying
billions in tax for years finally face the music. No, what he
means is massive cuts in pensions, wages, social spending and
government jobs for the mass of the Greek people. That's
what counts as being courageous in Mr Trichet's book.

Do Trichet and Papandreou really think the Greek people
are going to take this lying down? I don't think so.

13 Dec 09

While the stock markets were panicked by the news from
Greece, for others it offers a big money making opportunity.
It may seem perverse, but, in their world, it does make
perverted sense.

The banks have now turned their debt disaster into a huge
money making scam. Now that governments are on the hook
and broke, they are having to come back to the same markets
they helped to 'stabilize'. Those markets can now bleed one
country after another for every penny they can get.

The most profitable game in town at the moment is a
relatively new one: it's called Front-Run the Bailout, and it
has been growing in importance to the financial world over
the last six months.

Here's how I think the game is being played. First, you identify
a large debt problem. Then, out of one side of your mouth,
you start to make dire, 'expert' predictions and warnings
about how serious this debt problem could become. Out of
the other side of your mouth, you offer to buy the debt or to
insure it against the event of default.

The more dire you make your warnings, the cheaper it gets for you to buy the debt for yourself, and the more you can charge others to insure it. You keep stoking the pressure. Then comes the critical moment in the game: that's when you have to convince the government(s), in your role as expert advisor – who's 'only trying to help' – that if this debt were to default, then the cost to the government, and the risk of an even bigger problem in the long run, would be far higher than the cost of stepping in and back-stopping the lot – NOW.

To win, you need to make absolutely sure the governments are convinced that paying is feasible (with a bit of austerity) and that not paying would be the end of civilization. When Brown, Obama or Trichet, whoever they are, agree to pay up, BINGO! You scoop up a profit the likes of which normal business acumen could never hope to achieve.

Greece is now on the hit list. The more the Greek government wobbles the better the profit could be. The trick is to work the panic enough but not too much. The goal is to rattle confidence. Make the EU think it could be split. Make Germany think that it should offer to help Greece. If it works, those front-running the bailout will soon feel the euros of profit come rolling in. The UK is also on the list. The election makes it a tasty prospect for next year.

And who will be some of the people betting against us? That's right, our banks with the bailout money we gave them.

18 Dec 09

While Trichet is urging the Greek government to make drastic cuts in spending, an insight into how differently the EU treats the banks came today.

As part of their preparations for unwinding their financial emergency measures, the European Central Bank (ECB) has just asked all the banks who previously sold them assets in return for bailout money to provide 'clearer information' about the nature and real worth of those assets.

Think about that for a second.

This means the ECB has just admitted it is holding assets in return for bailout cash, but it has no clear idea what the assets are, nor what, if any, real worth those assets have. In short, the ECB accepted bundles of sealed brown paper envelopes stuffed with bad smelling mystery paper, and they never even asked to see inside. In return, they handed over hundreds of billions of OUR money.

I trust neither the bankers nor those who claim to be regulating them. They are all of the same financial class. They are all wealthy beyond your dreams, and they all believe with a true zealot's unshakable faith in their financial ideology. Our futures are being systematically slaughtered upon the altar of that faith.

Got a joke for you to lighten the gloom.

A bunch of ostrich bankers are standing around in the desert worried about the dreadful mess they have made. Suddenly, they see a cloud of dust coming towards them and know it is the ostrich bank regulator. In a panic, they do what ostriches and bankers do: they all stick their heads in the sand.

The ostrich regulator comes charging up, stops, looks around a little perplexed and then asks, 'Where did everyone go?'

Best I could do in the circumstances.

22 Dec 09
As the vultures move in, it looks more and more like the UK could suffer a ratings downgrade in the coming year.

Do you think the bond market is going to care? They just want their money, and they don't care what our government has to do to give it to them. Without significant growth, the only way the British government will be able to pay its debts is if it amputates whole limbs of government spending. Cuts and more cuts will be made, but the banks and the markets will care nothing. For them, government cuts are sideshows to the main act: their profits and their bonuses.

And what will we do? Find some poor sod to point a finger at? It seems to me the measure of the bankers' victory will not just be how much of our wealth they can take, but how easy it is for them to use the levers of political and media power to make sure that we now turn on each rather than on them.

The list of easy targets and handy whipping boys and girls is almost endless: public sector workers with big fat pensions, pen-pushing civil service bureaucrats, job-shy single mums, privileged middle-class students, obstructive trade unionists, benefit scroungers, job stealing immigrants. Do you recognise someone? Will we set to fighting each other for the scraps that are left on the floor? Will the bankers and financial aristocracy fade from our minds? No thought that we shouldn't have bailed out these parasites? No thought that all of the political class, every man jack of them, has betrayed us?

We must realise and remember that the *only* reason our borrowing is suddenly out of control, and the *only* reason there won't be enough money for schools and retirement, for heating for our parents and for university places for our children is because it has been taken from us by our political leaders and given to those whose wealth and power they bow down to.

And make no mistake, it isn't over. The bankers have a taste for this effortless pillaging. Why should they stop when we are so craven before them?

Have a happy Christmas, the bankers will.

CHAPTER 10

The Debt of Nations

1 Jan 10

If 2009 was the year of the private debt crisis then I believe 2010 will be the year of the national debt crisis. Our central banks are beginning to drown, and they know it. That is because the last year has been spent transferring the private debts of the banks onto the public purse. Those countries that bailed out their banks now have huge national debts *plus* the private debts of banks *and* the interest payments on both. That is the idiocy that has passed for policy on both sides of the Atlantic.

The problem is the losses are not contained or stopped, and the ability to borrow and print them away is decreasing. This means we are now, even more, at the whim of the bond markets. This will create such volatility and uncertainty that major dislocations and defaults are inevitable.

Those fools who spend their time gazing at parochial indicators, such as UK house prices and high street sales figures, will get swept away by the wave they never see coming.

4 Jan 10

New year celebrations are out of the way, and our experts are starting to get excited about signs of recovery. This is a bit like looking at one little part of your body, not finding any spots just there, and concluding you are on the mend, ignoring the weeping pustules spreading all over your back and down your legs. I know I am in a shrinking minority who do not think it is all on the mend. But I don't, I really don't.

Let's look at some of the facts. In the US housing market one in ten prime mortgages is now either behind or defaulted. That's *prime* mortgages: mortgages given to America's most creditworthy buyers. If they are in trouble, what does that say about everybody else?

At the same time, the Option ARMs are piling up like corpses in a ditch. They just keep on dying. Mass graves are hard to hide after a while. $389bn to reset and recast before 2012. It starts this summer, and nothing is going to stop it. Current estimates are that 63% of them will go BOOM at current estimates. If that isn't enough, there are the problems in commercial real estate that are crippling major cities from New York to Phoenix. It's the same story everywhere: no rents, no buyers.

If you believe that a big rise in US property prices is an essential part of getting us out of this mess then what does all that say about our future prospects?

And that's just the US: look at Japan. The new Japanese government has announced a £630bn spending spree. That brings Japanese debt to GDP ratio to 195%! Expect the rating agencies to start making noises about this. What happens when the world's second largest economy starts down the road to downgrades on its debt? Japan is the wildcard in this game.

Then there are Canada and Australia. What do these two have in common? Insane private debt levels. Australians now owe more than 100% of GDP. Each of them owes over $70k. Debt on mortgages, credit cards and loans stands at $1.2 trillion and is up 71% in only five years. Canada is in similar trouble. They have a very nasty housing bubble that will burst fairly soon.

Finally there is the UK. Two of the largest bond investors, PIMCO and BlackRock, have said they will NOT buy UK government bonds in 2010. Not just that, they have said they will become net sellers instead. If Alistair Darling thinks that is a big vote of confidence in the future of the UK economy then he really should see about changing the tint on his spectacles.

6 Jan 10

More rose-tinted news came this morning. According to a bright and breezy report in the Guardian, 'Investors snapped up a £4bn auction of government bonds today, defying critics who have warned that so-called gilts could be shunned over concerns about the public finances.'

The auction for short-term debt is over-subscribed? Great! The real story is that investors are selling long-term debt and buying short-term debt instead. It's something I have been trying to highlight for over a year now. It's the classic response of investors becoming nervous about a county's long-term ability to pay its debt.

Is this a problem? I think it will be. Much of our debt is still very long-term. But as you borrow more and more the more the pressure to issue shorter term grows because the people who are buying the debt start to get nervous and want debt that is going to be paid back sooner. And pay it back we must. When the term of the gilt expires the government has to return the whole capital sum it borrowed. That's how gilts work.

Short-term debt makes the whole thing unstable. Our government, like all others, will have spent that money, so they will have to borrow yet more from someone else, at whatever price, to pay off the sum of the original gilt. If they don't, KAPUT! Britain goes bust.

I think this means we haven't seen the end of quantitative easing. I am sure the Bank of England will try to hold off as long as possible, but eventually it will find the pressures too great. Restarting QE will strike the bond markets as an admission that the Bank of England is not in control of its own money, but not restarting risks no-bids in their debt auctions, which is an even riskier scenario. Whichever route we take it is not going to be pretty.

21 Jan 10

Confirmation of the dire state of our national finances came today. Official figures show that UK government borrowing for December was the highest in recorded history. National debt as a proportion of GDP was also reported to be at the highest levels since records began.

It is worth bearing in mind, when thinking about this, that it's not actually how much debt, nor even debt as a percentage of GDP, which counts for the market. What matters to the market is your ability to pay it back. It is quite possible to have a national debt of 100% or more of GDP if you also have a massive engine to pay it off. The US can ride larger borrowings because they sit, or at least sat, on a V12 production engine. We, on the other hand, have an ailing two-stroke lawn mower.

The problems arise when the bond market begins to feel a country's level of debt is greater than their productive capacity to pay it back. That puts the UK, particularly, in a double bind. The largest part of our earning capacity has been the financial sector, but it is this very sector that is causing us to borrow so much.

What do we do when the banks come back to us later this year, and the next, needing yet more bailout money? Pay up and hope above hope they make bigger profits and get richer and richer, or refuse to pay and watch as the billions we have spent so far are simply flushed away?

The governments are now damned if they do and damned if they don't. That is the entirely predictable outcome of their earlier, stupid 'save the banks whatever the cost' policies.

22 Jan 10

Those stupid 'save the banks' policies are also why, despite all Obama's recent tough talk about a need for a 'clampdown on the banks', I don't think we will ever see any *serious* banking reform.

You can almost hear all the bankers' lobbyists frantically telling Obama, Brown and Darling that if we don't allow them to make large profits from casino banking, they won't be able to pay us back. Not only that, they will no doubt be saying they won't be able to withstand the next round of losses and will therefore need more of our money to survive.

Governments, they will tell our leaders, must:

- NOT regulate financial products, risk-taking, or bonuses in any way.

- NOT bring back mark-to-market accounting rules.

- NOT reduce leverage at financial institutions.

- NOT allow any large financial institutions to go bust.

- NOT properly audit the central banks.

- NOT allow openness and transparency in reporting of any part of the financial situation lest it cause a 'loss of confidence'.

They will also, of course, say that governments MUST be ready to take on any level of sovereign debt necessary for further bank bailouts while, at the same time, reducing national debt levels by cutting social spending, pensions, benefits, education, health and wages.

That is what the bankers will be arguing today … and in a way they will be correct. They will simply be laying out the logic of our leaders' earlier idiocy. No matter who is in power, the bankers will expect their commandments to be obeyed. That is the nightmare we have been led into.

That is why there is not going to be any banking reform. There may be some window dressing, but that is all it will be.

25 Jan 10

The news the 'green shoots' brigade has been waiting for came today: we are now officially out of recession. Don't you feel so much better? Nearly a trillion in government lending, bailouts and insurance guarantees; £2000 hand-outs to car buyers; a 2.5% cut in VAT across the board, and what do we get? 0.1% growth! That's not good news: that's a big problem.

Let me try to explain why. So far it is only the bailout money that has prevented the banks defaulting on any payments. Unless they get a massive reinflation in the values of their assets, they will still need that flow of cash from us to keep them solvent. Low or even normal growth simply won't do.

Just as low or normal growth won't do for the banks neither will it do for the government. We have taken on massive debts to bail out the banks, but because unemployment is high and industrial production is low our income is not keeping pace with our growing outgoings. And that's before the banks start demanding more.

For this plan to have ever worked it needed bubble-like growth because it was only insane levels of growth that would reinflate the value of the banks' assets *and* provide the government with the income to pay off the national debt. Anything less and the plan sinks. And sink it is going to because, far from getting those levels of growth, whatever 'fragile recovery' does exist is actually teetering on the edge of a cliff.

Look at the evidence. Consumer spending in the largest consumer market, America, is still declining. New house sales have declined, again. Commercial real estate defaults are continuing to grow, and losses from Alt-A and Option ARM mortgages will only start to get serious this spring.

Then there is Ireland. It looks like they are edging closer and closer to a bank collapse. All their banks are in deep, deep trouble. Their credit ratings are slipping and borrowing costs ramping up. There are political rumours of a bank closure. It could be Anglo Irish or Bank of Ireland that is very close to going under. They are just rumours, and rumours are cheap to spread, but such talk is itself damaging. If there is not a strong, global reinflation to speculative price levels then Ireland will implode.

Elsewhere the signs are equally bad. Greek debt is way out of control. If Greece doesn't amputate – not cut or trim but amputate – public spending on salaries and pensions, they default. If they do default, it will reverberate like a shot in Sarajevo. Not even China will now buy Greek debt.

The Chinese themselves spooked the whole Asian market as soon as they even spoke about reigning in their own banking and housing bubble – a bubble that will burst if they don't do something about it.

And then there is Japan. As I have said before, I really think Japan is the wildcard that nobody seems to be talking about much. Consumer spending is at a low not seen for over two decades, and their debt is getting out of control. Up until now, the Japanese government has been able to sell its debt to its own people and financial institutions. Not any more. The era when the people of Japan bought their government's debt with their own savings is winding down. The Japanese people are no longer flush with savings, and what they have is already invested in Japanese government bonds. At the same time, the Japanese banks are looking to stop buying government debt. That's happening while the cost of insuring Japan's debt has skyrocketed. Far from dragging the world economy up, Japan could be one of the weights that pulls it down.

Two other things could hasten a lurch down more quickly. The first is if the Fed, in particular, needs to prop up its debt sales by scaring money back out of stocks and into treasuries. Given the mind-boggling amounts of debt the US absolutely must sell in the next year alone, they may have to do this.

The second factor speeding up a downward turn is if any of the bigger players in stocks start to edge towards the exits. There are hints that this is already afoot. Take a look at two of the big PIMCO funds. Over the last few days, two of the big ones have been selling huge volumes and been willing to take significant losses. PIMCO has said, straight out, that they are looking for safety above any return at all.

In the light of all this, can anyone seriously expect that the recovery is going to provide the level of growth they need in the time they need it to happen? The brutal truth is this recovery was always built on government paper stimulus, and when that goes so does any so-called recovery.

The only other course is to do what we should have done in the first place: stop claiming the crisis is merely a matter of liquidity, and admit the crisis is one of solvency. Whatever they might say, the banks aren't fine and their assets are worth a fraction of what they claim. They will continue to be worth little for the foreseeable future.

The problem now is that even if we do come to our senses and stop the insane transfer of public wealth to the financial class, we will have to face the loss of everything we have spent so far. At some stage, this is the tragic fact we are all going to have to confront. At the moment, all we are doing with our current policies is paying a higher and higher price for putting off the day of reckoning.

28 Jan 10

Despite all the evidence to the contrary, everyone is expecting that the US is going to record strong growth. I have to say, I now take US figures with the same caution as Greek ones. What growth there has been so far is mostly in banking and defence. If you think that is how to build a recovery that will feed, clothe, educate and look after you and your children, then we don't live in the same reality.

I don't think I can remember a figure the US government has released in the last year that wasn't, if one is being kind, at first 'massaged' up and subsequently 'revised' down. What is interesting is that the massaged up figures always lead to an immediate jump in the markets, while the revised down ones are never spoken of.

To give a concrete example: orders for durable goods, a sign of where manufacturing is headed, were heralded in

November as having risen 0.2%. The recovery was here! All 0.2 % of it. The market ramped up, but then, quietly, the figure was revised down to a 0.4% decline!

That's one of the reasons I don't think the next set of figures will be as strong as the experts predict.

29 Jan 10

I thought the growth figure wouldn't be as high as the experts were predicting, and in fact it was better. The preliminary figure is 5.7%. I still expect this to be revised down, but even revised it will be high.

Call me a curmudgeon, but I can't help feel that most of the growth will turn out to be government stimulus led and not sustainable. When that gets withdrawn, as it did from house building, growth will disappear. And withdraw it they must because they simply cannot afford to carry on.

One of the reasons I think we will see the stimulus being withdrawn is found in other figures released today. AIG, bailed out so far to the tune of $182bn, now needs another $24bn. The rate of loss has been $1bn per week for the last six weeks. And the cause? Losses on commercial real estate loans. AIG can't sell the loans and so is stuck with the losses. The figures also tell you that the rate of losses – at least in AIG's portfolio – is considerable to say the least.

This means that the long awaited crunch in commercial real estate is happening and was not a figment of the fevered imagination of doomsters like myself. AIG was far from alone in buying the stuff. The Fed itself bought $1.2 trillion dollars worth at face value and used up most of its liquid assets to do so. It now finds itself short of cash and yet holding assets it can't get rid of – assets that are now worth far less than they originally paid.

The effect of that cash shortage will soon spill over into the residential mortgage market. At some stage pretty soon, the Fed will have to stop buying up Fannie and Freddie paper because they just won't be able to afford it. The problem is no one else wants it. As it stands, the Fed is the only buyer in town. Last year alone they bought $1.3 trillion. It is that cash which keeps money flowing to the banks for new mortgages. What happens when it stops?

Well, the likelihood is Fannie and Freddie freeze, and the US mortgage market grinds to a halt. Then what? At the very least we will see a sales nose-dive, a fall in prices and, more than likely, a flood of foreclosures and another major round of bank write-downs and possible defaults. Any growth that has taken place will disappear like castles in the sand swept away by the incoming tide.

Those who believe in the recovery, and the plan behind it, will no doubt ask me what level of stock market recovery, and what news of employment picking up, is required for me to admit I have been wrong?

My answer to them is that stock levels don't convince me of anything except that those who have been given money by our governments are making money with it. I don't see that as proof of a recovery, but rather as compelling evidence that the financial economy is actually separating from the rest of the economy. Only a sustained increase in employment and household consumption would help convince me that there was a real recovery underway.

In turn, I would ask them what level of national debt, and level of yield on that debt, will make them admit that all we have done is transform one crisis into another, much larger one? What will it take for them to see that we haven't avoided Armageddon, but just paid a very high price for putting it off for a while?

1 Feb 10

It is a question I have asked before, but who exactly is buying up all the sovereign debt? It's a simple question. Trillions of dollars, euros and pounds have been issued. Who had the spare money to buy it all?

Last year the Chinese went from $713bn to $801bn and then down to $789bn. Basically a holding pattern. Certainly not the huge buyer they have been. The Japanese increased their dollar debt from $626bn to $757bn. Not bad for a country with nearly 200% GDP debt of its own.

The real eye-opener was the UK. Sit down for this. Figures from the Fed show that between November '08 and November '09 the Bank of England more than DOUBLED our holdings of US debt. We went from $132bn to $277bn. That means we bought $145bn in new dollar debt! And we did this while our own borrowing got so out of hand we were warned to stop or face a credit downgrade.

Why do this? Where did we get the money? I think it could be a way of hiding the amount of quantitative easing and creating the illusion that there is a real market for national debt. The US can say that they had no trouble selling their debt, while the British can claim to hold apparently solid assets on their balance sheet. What neither, of course, would mention was that all they each got in return was more empty debt. It provides the illusion that behind all the new debt there is a solvent and worthy creditor. If I'm correct, there is no solvent creditor behind it at all. Nothing. Nobody. Just a vault of empty promises.

That should guarantee a good night's sleep for everybody.

6 Feb 10

Oh dear! This is where things could start getting very nasty, very quickly. Greece looks like she is on the very verge of default. The country has to cut its debt NOW, or the bond market will shut them out, and their banks will go down. But it isn't just Greek banks that will suffer. German, Spanish, French and Irish banks are all tied up with Greek debt. There are unknown credit default obligations on Greek debt with some of Europe's largest banks that could well blow them apart. The Irish banks alone stand to loose €6bn. They cannot absorb such a loss. The French and Spanish banks likewise. So either Greece and its banks, both national and private, are bailed out or it's BOOM, BOOM, BOOM.

That's why a lot of the talk now is about the possibility of a German bailout for Greece. The problem is that discussing Greek debts in isolation from the debts of other European nations is as daft as assiduously putting ointment on one sore while ignoring the others clustered round it. Greece is just an early bird pustule that heralds the eruption of others.

Portugal and Spain are two that look just ripe to burst. The 'left wing' minority government in Portugal tried to get debt cutting measures passed but was defeated. Instead, an utterly brilliant alternative was tried: let the regions and municipalities try to sell their own debt. Avoid a national debt problem by having lots of regional debt problems. Five gold stars for that piece of idiocy.

And then there is Spain. Back in October 2008, the Spanish government guaranteed €100bn of bad debt for its banks. That bad debt is worse now because their property values are still declining fast. Their regions also took to issuing their own debt. At some stage soon this is all going to bite. We may see evidence at Spain's next bond auction. If they get a no-bid then we all take a big step closer to the cliff edge.

This is the problem Germany faces. If they agree to bail the Greeks, what do they do about the Portuguese and the Spanish? Will they be expected to bail them out in turn?

It's a very nasty conundrum. If they don't bail the Greeks and Greece defaults, the domino effect in credit default swaps and direct bank exposures means there is a high risk other debtor nations will fall over in quick succession. The trouble is, if they do bail Greece out, the others will also expect to be saved when they themselves reach the precipice.

That's why there's no easy answer, not least when you realise that Germany has problems of its own. In 2010 Germany needs to borrow around €340bn. This figure includes old bonds that mature and short-term debt that needs to be rolled over. Germany is an economic powerhouse, but €340bn isn't chicken feed, especially when a lot of their export customers in Euroland are getting considerably poorer.

And that isn't the only problem. The key thing to remember about many European countries is that, while national debts are what hit the headlines, state and municipal debts often get forgotten. Portugal falls into this category, so, importantly, does Germany.

Last year, the German government estimated that as much as €500bn in toxic debt was festering in the German *Landesbanks*. These are banks that are majority owned by the German states, but their debts are not counted as German national debt.

So far, Germany has done what the US did with some of its troubled banks. Saxony LB was saved (bought) by another larger *Landesbank* just like Washington Mutual was 'saved' by JP Morgan. But these are stopgap measures. The fact they have to face is that the *Landesbank* debts are not going away. In some cases, they are worse off than they were a year ago. Time for them is money, in the negative sense.

If, on top of all this, you then add a minimum of €200bn which is still rotting in Germany's private banks, you have the second largest dung heap of illiquid or structured toxic assets outside the US.

That's why I don't think a German bailout is, by any means, a done deal. Germany simply can't afford endless bailouts. If it tries, it will enter a Japan style lost decade. Japan is already there and sinking.

Before there is any bailout of Greece, Germany needs to get enshrined in pan-European precedent that debtor countries will be forced to rein in debts. That means Portugal, Spain, Ireland and others must be forced to make cuts now. Those cuts are bound to meet lots of resistance from the people of those countries. That, in turn, means the only way the sovereign debt crisis doesn't blow up all over Europe is if the police forces of each country ensure people do what they are told and accept the cuts in services and attacks on their living standards.

In Ireland the people are currently trotting along quietly, but Greece is another matter entirely. Farmers are blockading roads, students are on the streets and the biggest unions are preparing to strike. What will happen in Spain and Portugal? Will their people walk meekly to their fate like the Irish, or will they fight like the Greeks?

A summer of discontent beckons – and that will only be the beginning.

CHAPTER 11

The Balancing Act

11 Feb 10

Jean-Claude Trichet, the head of the European Central Bank, 'reassured the markets' today, saying that he would join in monitoring Greece's cuts and help '*planning* new ones if necessary.'

From one perspective, I suppose this sounds fine. Those rascally Greeks are in debt, so the ECB keeps a close eye on them. Nothing wrong with that you might think. But, wait a minute. Last I heard, Greece was a democratic, sovereign nation where the people had the right to decide what they did – even if that meant deciding to default on their debts. What we are now hearing is that the unelected head of a bank is going to plan new cuts 'if necessary.' Is that if the Greek people think it's necessary, or if he thinks so?

In a democracy you can hope to do something about unelected officials dictating which services should be cut, but suddenly Greece finds it has become democracy *lite*. When you are in debt it's your bank manger who owns you, as Greece is finding out.

Let's be frank. Greece took on vast, unpayable debts and lied about them for years and years while becoming more and more insanely over-stretched. Finally, they imploded under a weight of bad debts and empty assurances so large they could not pay them. Not good. I think Greece has a case to answer and some work to do to sort itself out.

But, we should remember, this is exactly what every major bank in the US and the UK did, and are still doing, to this very day. Exactly the same things. What's more, it was our accountants and bankers who 'advised' and 'helped' the Greek government to be more economical with the truth than they were with their accounts. The banks did everything the Greeks did, and more, yet while the bankers were bailed out, with few strings attached, the Greek people are being made to pay brutally for any 'help' they receive.

Isn't there something ugly, perverted and deeply wrong about that? Doesn't it tell you something about who has power and who doesn't?

Contrast Latvia, Estonia, Ireland, Iceland, and Greece, on the one hand, with Citigroup, AIG, JP Morgan, Wells Fargo, Lloyds, RBS, and Société Générale, on the other.

Latvia has been forced by the IMF and its creditors to cut spending so savagely it has had to close numerous schools and hospitals. The cuts have also pushed the economy into an even deeper and longer recession. In two years of IMF austerity, Latvia's GDP has collapsed 25%, and unemployment is now over 20%. It will be 2015 before it even returns to where it was in 2006, and that's if you believe the IMF experts.

The banks, on the other hand, are not going to be forced to accept any austerity measures. In the US and UK, the banks are adamant that any punitive actions against them, any regulation of their bonus culture or their risk-taking and speculating, would precipitate a further downturn. Yet these very same bankers are icily sanguine when it comes to punitive cuts to nations and people. The bailout of AIG has ALREADY COST MORE THAN THE PROPOSED BAILOUT OF GREECE, yet there have been NO austerity measures for AIG! Bonuses flow like wine!

Why one necessary strategy for the banks themselves and the opposite for people and nations? We can agree that if the Greeks want money then their creditors should have a say. But then why do we have no say over the bankers who needed and got our money?

Look at wages. The Greek people are being told they must accept drastic pay cuts and have their pensions flayed in public. Bankers, on the other hand, are not even to have minimal over-sight of their bonuses. What's more, we are informed that if we want bankers to work hard, we must not cut or curb their already lavish rewards. We ordinary people, however, are told we must work harder for less money, less security and less hope for our children. People must lose their jobs. Bankers, however, mustn't be upset by talk of regulations lest they all leave. Purging for the people, soft oils and baths for the wealthy.

What Marie-Antoinette would give to be alive now.

16 Feb 10

The extent to which the banks themselves connived in trying to hide Greece's debt problems is becoming more and more apparent. Many people have known about this for a long time, but it is only now, when Greek debt has been dragged kicking and squealing into the spotlight, that sounds of disapproval are being heard.

From 2001 onwards a number of the big banks, including Goldman, JP Morgan, Citigroup, Deutsche Bank and PNB

Paribas (note the German and French banks included in this list), helped the Greek government to hide the actual level of government debt from the EU by using what are known in financial jargon as Special Purpose Vehicles (SPV).

Essentially this involved moving the debt from one column in the country's accounts to another less public one whilst getting money up-front to make the country's debts seem smaller. Deutsche and Paribas arranged one SPV for Greece called *Atlas* valued at €2bn. Goldman arranged another called *Titlos* worth €5.1bn. *Titlos* is the one now in the headlines. If you can imagine making your mortgage seem as if it were money you had in the bank, rather than money you owed, you are well on the way to understanding this seemingly arcane area of national finance.

In Greece's case, the subterfuge was actually quite laughable as the ECB and Eurostat (the official financial statistics compiler) were both well aware of the deals but did nothing. Now, however, it seems the Greek chickens are coming home to roost.

Like many such deals, so long as the debtor has a 'good' rating from Fitch or Moody's then they don't need to post actual collateral. There are, however, clauses in the deals that can trigger payments. Get a downgrade and BOOM. This is what might happen to Greece. On top of its other debts, it could have to stump up €5bn immediately; that's €5bn it simply doesn't have. In that case, Germany might, at the very least, have to post the collateral for them. The problem is if Germany does this for Greece to cover *Titlos*, how many more will they have to buy out?

Greece was not alone in having SPVs. Portugal, we know, has them. Spain probably does as well. I would think it is a good bet that Ireland, as the home to many SPVs, also has its fair share. This is what makes the German bailout anything but easy. Bail one, they may have to bail them all. The Germans simply have no idea of how many SPVs might be waiting for them in the dark.

19 Feb 10

Yet more evidence of the umbilical link between the big banks and the parlous state of Greek finances came to light yesterday. The head of the Greek government's Debt Management Agency resigned. Can you believe they actually have a 'Debt Management' Agency? They must be a crack outfit! The Dad's Army of the financial world. These are the people who managed to work with Goldman Sachs and JP Morgan to arrange many of the SPVs and other aspects of Greece's finances which have caused so much trouble.

It turns out that the new person in charge is Petros Christodoulou, former head of private banking at the National Bank of Greece. Got a sinking feeling yet? You should, because before joining the Central Bank Mr Christodoulou was head of derivatives at JP Morgan, held a similar position at Credit Suisse, and... yes you guessed it, Goldman Sachs. The very same banks that 'helped' the Debt Management Agency with the country's finances.

That's what the market calls bringing in a clean broom!

20 Feb 10

If Greece is slowly turning to farce, it seems as though we may have a horror show on the cards in the US where it looks like there is a real bloodbath coming in commercial real estate.

How much blood? Well, the Congressional Oversight Panel have had a look and estimate $300bn in losses in the next few years. This is on $1.4 trillion in loans coming due. Given some of the write-downs that have already taken place have been up to 50%, this is a fairly conservative estimate. But, even at such conservative levels, the panel see it as posing a 'systemic risk'.

The systemic risk is not just the amount of the losses: it's where they happen. Commercial real estate is held mostly in mid-sized and regional banks. The commercial loans they hold are starting to drop like diseased fruit all over the States. I think there might be a feeding frenzy coming, a grotesque orgy of bank cannibalism, with the big boys feeding on their smaller country cousins.

The big banks have already been declared too big to fail, and they have the ear of Washington, so whatever happens they know they will be looked after. The regional banks aren't so lucky. They are not too big too fail, and they don't have the same political connections.

The collapse of these banks will cripple lending in their area, but it will also open the way for the big banking vultures to swoop down and greedily pick over the corpses of their banking cousins. The problem really gets going in 2011, so you have time to buy in the Party 7 and settle down for the show.

Just because the value of commercial assets has plummeted doesn't mean they are worthless. Many will still have some value and produce some cash flow. Not enough to save the regional banks holding the assets at full face value, but if you can pick up the assets for a song then there will be money to be made. It could be that the regional banks will be unceremoniously slaughtered so that the big banks can gorge themselves on the remains. Local misery, but joy for the big players.

It may also be that the big banks will benefit in a second way from this collapse. In the long run, this could be even more important. Regional banks have the modern equivalent of banking gold: depositors. As banks collapse, depositors are concentrated in those that survive. Wouldn't the big banks love to find they could reap a rich harvest of depositors' cash? It would change the shape of American banking, further concentrating power in fewer and larger national banks. The too-big-to-fail banks would become even bigger and have even more power over their regulators.

Let's see what happens.

21 Feb 10

US banking troubles or not, everyone in Europe is still waiting for Angela Merkel to answer the $254bn dollar question. The problem for all concerned is that she is not sure of the answer.

Here is what she does know. Of the $254bn of Greek debt, $64bn has to be financed this year alone. Of that, $30bn must be sold by March–April. She also knows that about two-thirds of Greece's total debt is held by the banks of just three European nations: France €73bn, Switzerland €59bn and Germany itself with €39bn.

Now, these are not massive numbers, but large landslides usually start with small pebbles. Take France: that €73bn of Greek debt is 3% of its own GDP. Then look at just one comparison. Bear Stearns, which started the whole landslip in the first place, was just 2% of US financial holdings at the time.

Everyone knows this, which is why Greece, even though it is so small, worries them so much.

The way I think the EU and the banks will try solve the problem is to go for the 'Argentine solution'. When Argentina looked like defaulting a few years ago, its government agreed draconian cuts. Its creditors smiled happily and obligingly rolled over and 'restructured' critical debts. Disaster was averted. When it became clear that the Argentine government hadn't made the cuts, the storm clouds gathered again, and a similar buggers' muddle was agreed. This happened several times. After a while, it made everyone suspect that this 'smile and wave' solution was all it ever was. Just smile and wave boys while you buy some time. Eventually, it all went flump, but in banker and politician land 'eventually' always looks more attractive than now.

22 Feb 10

Here is another reason why they are all so worried by Greece. A report a couple of days ago in Frankfurter Allgemeine Zeitung shows how interconnected everything in this crisis really is. It also shows how the ripples might fan out. According to the German paper, AIG might have written credit default swaps on Greek debt. If that turns out to be true, then break out the imodium and tuck in those trouser legs. If AIG insured Greek debt, this means the US taxpayer will get part of the bill at least. Now, the amounts aren't that huge, but Americans are still smarting form AIG's last back-door bailout of Société Générale and Deutsche. If it now turns out they have to bail out more troublesome foreigners – and it's the 'have to' that hurts – then I think this will get nasty.

One of the reasons it will get nasty is because the big US banks are still clearly in trouble and putting their own demands on the Fed. It's not just commercial real estate, and it's not just the regional banks. You only have to look at what happened a couple of days ago. The Fed announced a 0.25% increase in the rate it charges the banks for overnight loans. When it did, the markets started shaking with fear. One quarter of one per cent and the whole stinking pile wobbles!

These are the banks that are supposedly now making multi-billion dollar profits. These are the banks hosing down their genius traders and analysts with billions of dollars in bonuses because they have supposedly done so very well! And yet one quarter of one per cent increase in overnight loan rate is enough to shake the whole thing and require the Fed to reassure everyone that this wasn't a sign of tightening in 2010!

Ignore their lies. The banks are still carrying massive undisclosed losses. They are still marking assets as worth far more than they could possibly fetch on the open market. That's why the bankers will still need our cash. Without it we could all be dancing on their graves.

25 Feb 10

Today we got yet another reason, if more were needed, for why the banks should be well and truly buried. RBS announced a £3.6bn loss and at the same time says it plans to payout £1.3bn in bonuses to its staff.

Of course, we all know what the excuse will be: 'If we don't pay large bonuses we can't attract or keep our top quality bankers.' To which the obvious response is to ask what top quality bankers? The imbeciles who got us in the mess in the first place? Let them go! 'But the investment broking arm made £5.7bn profits.' I can hear someone whine. So what? This is the very same arm, most likely the very same people, who made such disastrous losses that they would have put RBS and themselves out of business were it not for the billions we gave them.

And remember, those losses weren't made on fine loans whose failure was inexplicable. How much 'due diligence' do you think was actually involved? How many bankers seriously worried about the real credit worthiness of the loans? I don't believe many did because this would have slowed the flow of the bonus billions. Make loans you know the bank is too highly leveraged to cover should the loan default, and then cash the bonus and wipe your expensive shoes on any grunt from the street with the audacity to question you. The money they made, and the reputation of the 'smartest men in the room', was a function of leverage not brains. Given enough leverage a chimp can make money, as many did.

So all the City slickers can talk about 'profits' and 'creating wealth' when RBS no longer has over £200bn in worthless assets sitting on the public purse in the Asset Protection Scheme, and when it has paid back every penny we have given to them, with interest. Until then, they can get back under the rock they crawled out from under.

But, before they do, maybe they could let us know how many bankers in RBS will be speculating against sterling when the investment vultures decide we are the ones who look ripe for picking.

And people still ask me why I get so angry.

4 Mar 10

All eyes today are on the Greek bond auction. If the Greek government manages to sell its long awaited bond offering of €3-5bn of 10-year debt, there will be a sigh of relief. Crisis averted will be the cry. And of course it will be, for the moment, but only for the moment. The problem for Greece is that it will certainly have to pay a higher interest rate to refinance its debt than it was previously paying. Estimates are that it will probably have to pay around 6.5% on the new debt.

What this means, if the sale goes 'well', is that Greece will be able to celebrate 'successfully' getting into a worse state, with larger debts, than it was in before. This is analogous to getting a new and worse deal on your mortgage and then cracking open the champagne. Hurrah!

This is step one in what is known as the debt spiral. Step two goes like this. You have borrowed money, now you put it to work. The whole reason to borrow is to invest the cash in something productive and hope like hell that the return on the money is greater than the interest you are paying to borrow it. That is the basis of all borrowing.

But what if you don't, or can't, invest it in something that makes a profit? And don't forget, it can't be something a little bit profitable: it has to be something that makes a profit greater than the cost of borrowing. In this case, Greece has to make more than 6.5% return on that money. If it doesn't, Greece will have to borrow even more to cover the difference. And it will have to pay an even higher rate for that extra borrowing … and so it goes. That's how the debt spiral tightens.

Greece is going to have to make more than 6.5% profit on any money it borrows in an economy that will contract by at least 4% next year. How likely is that? Of course, the way you can find the cash to make the payments is to make larger cuts in other spending. But if you cut more elsewhere, your economy will contract. When it does, your tax take declines, which means even more borrowing or even bigger cuts.

And this is the scenario if things go well!

8 Mar 10

Greece had to pay 6.25% on its 10-year bonds, twice what Germany pays. Despite this, some are considering it a glowing success, and the IMF is now assuring the world that Greece will come through the crisis without the need for a bailout.

Can I just remind people that in 2001-02 the IMF also said, numerous times, that Argentina would also come through its financial problems. Until, that is, Argentina defaulted, devalued and generally imploded.

If you think this prediction was just a one-off mistake and feel confident the IMF are not blinkered by a dogmatic adherence to an unsuccessful economic theory and are *not*, I repeat *not*, in any way, a mouthpiece for their share holders – the largest of whom is the USA – then believe what they say about Greece.

If you are beginning to doubt their understanding and judgment, then there are very solid reasons for not believing what they say about Greece.

First, the level of debt repayment on its own will cripple any Greek recovery. Does anyone seriously think the Greek economy is going to grow at such a rate that it can pay off the level of interest it is going to be charged on its debt?

Second, so far the figures for the real level of Greek debt have been revised up every few months. There is every reason to expect this to continue because Greece, as we know, has lots of off-balance sheet debts. The same goes for Portugal and Spain. No one really knows the true level of debt out there.

Third, the IMF sees it as part of its job to 'restore confidence' in the economic system. The justification is that if people believe that everything is OK and getting better, then their actions will make it a self-fulfilling prophecy. That is because finance is about confidence, not truth. 'Restoring confidence', in my dictionary, is banker speak for lying. The only problem is when reality catches up with the lies – as it will do with Greece.

So, believe the IMF if you want. I think I will choose not to.

13 Mar 10

Even if the IMF feigns confidence in Greece, it must be having serious worries about the situation in Spain. Greece may or may not be containable – I don't think it is – but Spain definitely isn't. If Spain goes, they definitely will drag all of Europe with them.

Santander, in particular, has been bothering me for a while. I see it as the Spanish RBS.

Spain's banks were 'saved' by a 1999 law forcing them to hold higher reserves than most other European banks. They were also less exposed to US subprime than French, German and UK banks. Better capital reserves and low defaults rate have helped them trade, borrow and buy. Santander and others have benefited from this. But the longer and deeper the Spanish property crash becomes, the more miraculous it is that the Spanish banks continue to have so few losses. And this is where the problem is going to come from.

Let's take a comparison between Santander and the smaller Banco Bilbao Vizcaya Argentaria (BBVA). Both lent to Spanish developers to put up huge numbers of flats. BBVA is reporting 17% of its loans to developers as in doubt. Santander says only 8% of its loans are classified as bad. Now, BBVA could just be a very poorly run bank, or it could be the more realistic estimate of what faces Santander.

Even the Spanish Central Bank is beginning to question the numbers and is already examining if the country's banks are artificially postponing the reporting of their bad debts. If they are, and if, as expected, 2010 is a second year of contraction for Spain, losses should start to appear very fast. When they do, hold onto your hats because the ride down will be lightening fast.

15 Mar 10

Those still looking to China for salvation would do well to pay attention to what is happening in Spain. The bursting of the Spanish property bubble is why so many of Spain's banks are in trouble. There are many who believe the Chinese could be in for a similar fate but on a much, much bigger scale.

People tend to think because China has a totalitarian government that they are in control of everything. They are not. If China does have a plan, we shouldn't assume that anyone in China has any intention of following it.

Last year, the Chinese government wanted a stimulus for the economy, so they instructed their banks to lend. They did. In the first six months, Chinese local and state banks officially lent out $1.1 trillion (and a LOT more unofficially). The problem is the money was NOT lent out to those people and organisations the authorities wanted.

The central government had asked the banks to lend to local governments and enterprises. What they had had in mind was investment in viable businesses that might make things people wanted to buy. Instead, out in the country, local officials, local bankers and aspiring middle-class investors all colluded to invest in, build, and hope to sell on, a bubble of empty properties which they expected would make them all rich or richer.

According to several leading China researchers in the West – Victor Shih of Northwestern University, Kenneth Rogoff of Harvard, and James Chanos, a hedge fund manager – there is now a vast amount of debt that is never counted by the central government statistics nor by most international statistics. This debt was funnelled through investment vehicles specifically set up to get around laws designed to restrict levels of borrowing and risk-taking.

So, how adrift are official estimates of Chinese debt? According to the researchers, and others, the real level of Chinese debt could reach 96% of GDP by next year. The official IMF estimate is only 22%. That 74% difference is the measure of how much the central government is *not* in control of who is taking on what debt.

It seems clear to me that the era of absolute power of the party is over, but not because of students and workers in Tiananmen Square fighting for freedom of speech. The new revolutionaries aren't students, and the revolution isn't about a desire for democratic freedom. Those willing to challenge the party and ignore its decrees are the new, aspirant middle-class – people driven by greed and the desire for personal wealth. That greed is what is fuelling China's property bubble; it is also what will make the burst so spectacular when it comes.

16 Mar 10

All the events of the last few weeks in Greece, Spain, China and the US have made me think of a popular old music hall act.

At the beginning of the 20th century, an entertainer would spin a plate on the top of a tall, flexible pole, waggling the pole until the plate was spinning so fast it stayed balanced. The act was to see how many plates he could keep spinning at the same time. The longer it went on, the worse it got. The more poles and plates he added, the more perilously close to falling the plates would get. As they began to totter, he would rush from one to the other to rescue them.

There was an entertaining feeling of growing panic and inevitability as the forest of deftly spun plates gradually lurched into chaos. One hundred years later, I have the feeling that we are watching the same process with our financial system.

During the bubble years, we in the West created a dazzling forest of spinning debt and financial instruments. More and more plates of epic weight and size were raised higher and higher on spindly poles, spinning faster and faster, packed closer and closer. Then, one plate, Bear Stearns, crashed to the ground, and suddenly every plate began to slow and totter wildly.

Rather than let some plates fall and then start again – with perhaps a little more sense and a little less rampant gluttony and greed – our bankers and politicians decided that no effort or cost should be spared in keeping every plate aloft.

The plates are many and varied. The banks need to strengthen their capital reserves, but lending to business needs to increase. Greece, Ireland, Portugal and Spain mustn't default, but the EU needs to keep a grip on its spending. National debt must be sold, but interest rates mustn't go up. The stock market needs to keep going up, but money needs to flood the bond market. QE mustn't give rise to inflation, but the banks urgently need liquidity. Fannie and Freddie need to keep buying up mortgages, but the Fed needs to get a grip on its spending. China must keep buying debt but also keep a grip on its own real estate bubble. These are just some of the plates we need to keep spinning. There are many more.

One plate spinning nicely on its own won't do. So what if one spins faster by 0.3%? They must all be kept spinning: AIG, Fannie and Freddie, Greece, Ireland, RBS … the whole lot.

I have seen this act. You can never tell which plate will be the one to fall nor the moment when it does, but you know the longer it goes the worse it gets, and everyone knows how it ends. In the music hall that's what made it so much fun; this time might not be quite so enjoyable.

CHAPTER 12

A Tissue Of Lies

17 Mar 10

Greece is the future that awaits us all. That's why Merkel and Germany have made it clear that they have their eyes on the longer game. Greece doesn't. They are drowning today and that tends to concentrate the mind on the here and now.

But Merkel knows there is more to come. Spain, in particular, is headed for a major day of reckoning quite soon. There is only so long you can suffer 17% unemployment before the pressure of tax going in one direction, and unemployment benefits and property defaults going in the other, tear a ragged hole in the tissue of lies covering your bank and sovereign debts. That's why they all need to keep a full panic about Greek default at bay. If that fear takes hold, it will soon spread well beyond Greece.

To try and prevent this, I think Germany and the EU will offer Greece a series of staggered loans dependent upon a schedule of harsh austerity measures. The hope will be that the very existence of the loan facility will ease fears of a possible default and so encourage the bond market itself to do most of the lending.

Essentially this German strategy involves deploying an armada of words around a rowboat of commitment. Either Greece makes the cuts, and then the loans can be released if the bond market is still reluctant to lend, or they don't make the promised cuts, and all that Germany and the EU have lost is some hot air.

If the markets believe them, it might work in the very short-term. If or when they don't, they're done for.

Personally, I think the most likely scenario is warm words, followed by petrified inaction, followed by nasty crisis. That nasty crisis will be months away if the markets buy into the warm words at the European meeting on March 25-26. If they don't, and call Germany and Greece's bluff, then the end comes much quicker.

That said, I still doubt Germany will agree to a bailout until default and EU ruination are staring them incontrovertibly in the face. If Germany knuckles under, the political fallout in Germany will be immense. But if Merkel doesn't come to their assistance, Greece could find itself facing expulsion from the EU and then devaluation. Probably not quite what they all had in mind when they formed the single currency.

18 Mar 10

With all the mounting pressure from the markets, Germany and France are making noises that they would like to stop the predatory 'naked shorting' of sovereign debt that is stalking various indebted countries. Like all 'naked' transactions, the naked shorting of sovereign debt involves taking out insurance against the risk of sovereign default without actually holding that country's debt yourself. This is a bit like taking out insurance in case someone else's house burns down. A strange thing to do, but it clearly gives you a rather unhealthy interest in actually seeing their house burn down. The same goes for countries. If the country avoids default, you lose your money. Should the state of their economy mean they can't meet their payments and so default, then you are the big winner. Poverty and hardship for the people, millions for you. Bravo. Beatification awaits.

Despite being on the list of countries that will get shorted, Ireland and the UK are both against any regulation. The reason isn't hard to find. Ireland is the domicile for a very large number of financial vehicles used to speculate. Most of the rest are in the UK.

London and Dublin also share another desperate need. They both urgently require their financial markets to be the powerhouse of any recovery. It's a matter of life and death. Nothing else will make Brown's recovery plan work. He absolutely has to have massive growth, and fast. Only another even larger financial bubble can hope to do this. That's why all the talk of banking reform a few months ago was just that: talk. It's the same everywhere.

Look at what has happened in the US where Senator Dodd has just announced his proposals for reform. Unsurprisingly, Dodd has proved to be the dud we all thought he was.

One of the main proposals is for a 'consumer protection body'. A lion with balls? More like a castrated pet chihuahua. This impotent creature will be housed in the Fed – surprise, surprise – where its decisions will be overseen and vetoed by a committee made of representatives of the Fed. Given that the Fed themselves represent and are staffed by members of the big banks, you can see the slight problem with this set up.

Clauses about 'urging' (rather than demanding) the break up of these too-big-to-fail banks are weakened, even further, by saying this would only happen once an imminent systemic danger is 'clear'. And who will make this evaluation? It will, of course, be representatives from the Fed, the Federal Deposit Insurance Corporation (FDIC), the Securities Exchange Commission (SEC) and other toothless, gurning wonders.

This will, of course, ensure that nothing is done until the time for action has safely passed, and there is no longer any chance of a wealthy friend having to accept a loss when a perfectly good public bailout can be arranged.

Banking reform? I get wind just listening to them.

19 Mar 10

For those in any doubt that serious reform is needed, you have to go no further than the latest revelations to surface in the US concerning Lehman Brothers. 'Repo 105' is the name of the latest scandal.

A repo, if you don't remember, is a repurchase and resale agreement. It is when you agree to sell something, but the buyer agrees to sell it back to you at an agreed price on an agreed date. It's not a sale in the way that the corner shop sells sweets to children because the goods and the money are both going to be returned.

Central banks use them to withdraw money from the financial system to reduce inflationary pressure. They 'sell' illiquid assets to the banks in return for cash. That cash is then 'out' of the system and the money supply is 'tightened'.

Another slightly more dubious use is what Lehmans did in the run up to their bankruptcy, and it's suddenly causing the shit to fly. Those who might get caught in the spray are now desperate to be seen simultaneously surprised, outraged, horrified and indignant. What they certainly don't want to seem is complicit because what the clever boys and girls at Lehmans did was very naughty and very dangerous. It's a bit like playing with fireworks in someone's living room.

When Lehmans had to prove to a creditor, an auditor, a regulator, or taxman that they were solvent, they would repo what assets they could to another bank in return for cash. The other bank agreed because they knew they weren't really buying the assets, just temporarily holding them. All fine and above board so far.

What Lehmans did next is the naughty bit. They didn't show these sales as repos on their balance sheet but showed them as real sales. This made it seem as if they had found buyers for certain riskier assets and were correspondingly less leveraged and more solvent.

When the regulator went away, or the bank had published their quarter-end results, they would simply reverse the process. The whole thing would cost them whatever the other bank had charged them for the service. It seems that all through '07 and '08 Lehmans did this to make it look like they were less leveraged and had more cash than they actually had.

It would appear, however, that Lehmans may not have been alone. There have been suggestions that some other banks might have used repo 105-like tricks to help lessen their tax liability.

Here is how that might work in layman's terms. Imagine you had made a profit in your business and had all the cash in the bank. The taxman says he's on his way. You phone a friendly second-hand car dealer. He agrees to repo you a car. You give him your cash, and he gives you his car. The two of you agree to return car and cash – minus a small commission for his trouble – once the taxman leaves. You then carefully, and deliberately, show the transaction *not* as a repo but as having bought a car for the business. Suddenly, you have no profits to show the taxman. Your tax bill disappears and so does Her Majesty's inspector feeling downcast and troubled.

Now, this would probably be considered tax avoidance if you are middle-class, and tax cheating if you're working class. One would get a fine, the other a short stay at Her Majesty's pleasure. If you were a bank, however, and did something similar, you could get your well-heeled lawyers to argue that it is perfectly legal and all above board. Repo 105 would thus enter the banking lexicon as just another of the totally transparent, honest terms and practices such as 'impaired asset', 'non-functioning market', 'mark-to-model', 'liquidity problem' and 'stimulus' so beloved of our banking fraternity.

George Orwell would have marvelled.

23 Mar 10

Big news just coming in from China. China may be about to post its first trade DEFICIT since April of 2004. Now that is BIG news.

If, as I have been arguing for a while, China is focusing on building itself a stable domestic economy, instead of relying on exporting into a self-evidently unstable global economy, then there is no 'China's going to save us all' solution to this crisis. If Chinese economic growth is internal growth then this will not help the global economy in the way that the World Bank expects.

But, just as importantly, if China runs trade deficits then we simply do not have a buyer for our debt. It's as simple as that. If they start running a deficit, they will no longer have pots of foreign currency needing to be recycled back to the issuer, so they will no longer need to buy any US and European debt.

We need to stop listening to those who say China will save us. China is NOT here to save us from the catastrophe our financial class and their political servants have created.

24 Mar 10

Surprisingly, it doesn't seem Alistair Darling is too worried about what China is and isn't doing. 'Don't worry about my debts,' he essentially told the country today, 'I have looked into the future, and I see silver crossing my palm! I am expecting growth of 1 to 1.25% this year and – sly smile to the fool in the front row – 3% to 3.5% next.'

What universe is that going to happen in Alistair? Is it the universe where Greece is about to default or be bailed out by the IMF? Or where Portugal continues to gets its debt downgraded? Is it the universe where UK unemployment will increase as public sector jobs are slashed? Is this the same universe where even US debt sales have started to run into trouble? Thought not.

I suspect Mr Darling gets his growth forecasts from the same universe as Greece, the IMF and the EU get theirs. Every single one of them for the last two years has been wrong. Not a little bit wrong, but Grand Canyon, gaping-whole-in-the-ground wrong. As recently as October 2008, the IMF was forecasting that Greece in 2011 would have about 3% growth. By April of last year this was 'revised' down to about 1.2%, and by October 2009 it was down to about 0.8%. The EU estimates were hardly better.

Forecast sounds so much better than guess. But is it actually any more accurate? Evidence from the past suggests not. Forecasts are just the function of your model. If you assume certain things will create growth then, hey presto, feed the figures in and your model predicts growth. The result isn't based on the wondrous workings of the model somehow accurately mirroring the real world. It's based on the assumptions you fed into it in the first place. You get out what you want. And what do politicians and the financial class crave like a vampire craves blood? Growth! Everyone needs to forecast growth to save them having to face reality.

It's the only hope they have.

Do you know what the last resort of the debtor is? It is his assurance that he has a sure-fire winner in the 3.30 at Kempton. He's had a really good tip. So don't worry, he's good for it!

Believe at your peril!

25 Mar 10
Perhaps Alistair should feed some of the latest figures from the US housing market into his model and see what that comes up with.

According to the Office of Thrift Supervision (OTS), out of about $6 trillion worth of US mortgages for which it has figures 13.6% are behind with their payments (or delinquent, as they like to say in the US.)

Of that 13.6%, about $282bn worth of mortgages are 90 days or more behind. Generally, mortgages that far behind eventually default. But there is something more interesting. The sector getting worse fastest is the prime end. *Prime* US mortgages in what the OTS calls 'serious delinquency' jumped 16.5% in the last quarter alone. People who should never default are on the march to do just that.

That means big problems for their banks and ours. If the banks repossess and sell some of the houses in order to get some cash back, this will drive prices down even more. If prices go down, more home owners will be in negative equity, and around it goes. The knock on for us is that any securities written on these loans will drop in value, and the banks holding them will need more cash to plug the holes in their capital reserves. Of course, the banks could buy some of the properties themselves to keep prices up, but that requires lots of money they just don't have.

Whatever they say, the banks cannot survive without continued and renewed government bailouts. That is the reality. This means they will be telling us that *their* 'stimulus' can't be withdrawn while telling the government that *our* national debt is too high and must be brought under control.

It's their version of the Titanic rescue. Bankers first, women and children left to drown.

29 Mar 10

The reality of what this means is becoming crystal clear in Greece. This year alone, Greece has to sell €54bn and refinance another €20bn of national debt if they are not to go bankrupt.

Yesterday the Greek government offered €5bn in seven-year bonds to test the water. The bonds were giving a 6% return. This is twice the rate a bond buyer would get if they bought German bonds. Even so, the sale just scraped through. This suggests to me that the Greek bond rate won't be coming down anytime soon.

This is a big problem because Greece's recovery plan is based upon 'only' paying 4.5% interest. Anything above that will require more cuts. How on earth is one of Europe's weakest economies going to grow at anything near the rate needed to cover these costs? It simply isn't. Greece is in the early stages of a death debt spiral.

At the other end of Europe things aren't looking too peachy either.

In Ireland the financial situation is getting worse, not better. Ireland is about to bail out its two largest banks, Allied Irish and Bank of Ireland, again! The first bailout was €11bn. This didn't fix anything; it just bought some time. During that time another €12-15bn rotted away. The situation has reached critical again, and the new losses can't be hidden a moment longer. They have to be paid NOW.

If that wasn't enough, the Irish government is also preparing to take a lot more bad loans into its bad bank – up to €81bn! That should do wonders for their credit rating and borrowing costs! Of course, all this is happening while the government are pushing through huge cuts in public expenditure to the cheers of the financiers. At some point, hopefully soon, when the Rohypnol wears off, the Irish people will wake up and realise what is happening to them.

30 Mar 10

Greece is now getting worse from one day to the next. The bonds it only just managed to sell on Monday got dumped on Tuesday. So many of Monday's buyers wanted rid of them they were selling them for less than they paid just one day earlier. Not only that, on Tuesday Greece tried to sell €1bn in 12-year bonds. The auction failed. They only got bids for €390m even though the bonds came with 6% interest.

The question now has to be at what rate can they manage to get enough buyers? As I mentioned yesterday, the entire Greek plan depends on 'only' having to pay around 4.5% interest. Any more and they sink. This is why you keep hearing the Greek prime minister pleading for support from Europe to help bring their borrowing costs down. If they don't come down, let alone if they go up – as these failed auctions suggest they will – then there is no plan, and there will be no recovery.

1 Apr 10

If, after everything that has happened, there is anyone who still doubts we are being well and truly screwed by the financial class, just read today's Irish Times.

As we know, Anglo Irish Bank desperately needs another €10bn on top of the €12bn it has already had. What for? Is all that money going to boost the Irish economy and help ordinary Irish men and women? Not a chance. It is going straight to pay the bank's debts to its large investors.

The scandal is that the bank *does* have funds to pay these debts. According to the Irish Times, Anglo's 2009 accounts, published yesterday, showed that the bank had senior bonds worth €15 billion and subordinated bonds of €2.4 billion. These bonds could be used to absorb some of the vast deficit.

So why are the bondholders in Anglo-Irish not paying any of the loss? Usually what happens when a company has to pay its debts is that subordinated bonds get used against debts first. Then you move up the chain towards senior and super-senior. You use this money to pay the debts until all the debts are gone, or there is no money left. That's business and the risk the bondholders took when they invested. Profit by it; go to the wall by it.

Why, then, aren't Anglo-Irish bondholders sharing in the loss? The Irish Times offers this as the answer: 'The international financial markets regard senior debt as being as safe as deposits and burning these bondholders may harm the borrowing capacity of other Irish banks and the State.'

Who you might ask are these 'international financial markets'? They are, of course, the very financial class of people who include the senior bondholders. It couldn't be clearer. They see themselves, and their wealth, as sacrosanct. And it's not just an opinion, it's a threat! '... burning these bondholders may harm the borrowing capacity of other Irish banks and the State.'

Better to impoverish a nation, blight their lives and hopes, than to offend the financial class and 'harm' the borrowing capacity of other insolvent banks. Our politicians used to lift the robes of the priests to lick their arses clean. Now they seem to enjoy doing the same with their new lords and masters.

They tell us there isn't a choice. There was, and there is. You just have to get up off your knees to make the right one.

2 Apr 10

Greece and Ireland are the future no one wants to be marched into. It's a future of failed bond auctions, rocketing borrowing costs and massive cuts in public spending. But could even the mighty US be headed down the same road? For Greece 2010 could we read USA 2012? I wouldn't bet my mortgage on it, but you can be sure there will be bankers who will.

The US has absolutely huge debt sales. It has to sell around $139bn next week alone! But this last couple of weeks its bond sales of two, five and seven-year bonds were flops. They only sold because the Fed itself bought whatever was left. But foreign investors, and even foreign banks, kept their hands in their pockets. Now that is bad.

The immediate result is that the yield on US debt has started to march up. The rate on 30-year went up to 5%, which is a danger mark. It was only the Fed's own buying which pulled it back down to 4.75%. The 10-year, which is what underpins US mortgage rates, went up to 3.9%. This is a big problem because high mortgage rates will kill off any hope of a housing and commercial real estate recovery. Higher debts costs in general will also stifle any consumer spending and growth in the economy.

This puts the US authorities in a bind because if they want to bring rates down, they will have to force cash out of commodities and equities and back into bonds. Doing this, however, risks spiking the stock market down. I think Bernanke is hoping if they leave it long enough the optimism about a recovery will help the markets withstand the shock and continue up. Will it work? I don't think so.

8 Apr 10

While Bernanke ums and ahs about what to do in the US, it seems a few Greek banks could be seeing their last days.

'Commerzbank is pulling its repos from Greek Banks' might not be a headline to set the pulse racing, I admit, but it should be. That's because without repurchase and resale agreements to provide liquidity no modern bank can function.

According to a report on the Greek financial news site, BankingNews.gr, the German bank has decided the assets that the Greek banks had put up as collateral were not in fact worth what the Greek banks had claimed. This is *exactly* what happened in the run up to the collapse of Lehmans. Its counterparties also began to doubt the real value of the assets the bank was offering. Once that happened, Lehmans was dead in the water.

The problem for the Greek banks is that their government can't step in to help because it's virtually bankrupt itself. So any bailout means turning to Germany, France and Switzerland – the three nations whose banks have most to lose if there is a Greek bank collapse.

The Greek government has to hope that Germany, France and Switzerland calculate that the exposure of their own banks to Greek bank debt means that a bailout of Greece is essentially a bailout for their own banks. And that's what we have to realise. A Greek bailout is, for all intents and purposes, a bailout of the banks the Greek government owes money to.

If Greece were to default, one of the first things that would happen is that at least one major French bank would be blown out of the water. According to one leading hedge fund manager, a realistic estimate is that Greek debt could burn €35bn of French bank capital holdings. Could they survive that? No, at least not without a government or ECB bailout.

The German banks would similarly lose a vast amount, as would the Swiss.

British banks would not immediately suffer, but the effect on Spain and Portugal would be swift. One or more Spanish banks would teeter. Portugal would also lose one. Both countries would see their borrowing costs and insurance on their debt join the Greeks in the wilderness. That would start the destruction of the British banks. And if it turns out that AIG really did write a lot of credit default swaps on Greek debt then even the Fed might get hit for a large chunk of money.

As a result of all this, growth projections in all countries would collapse. That would mean cuts NOW. I could go on, but it would be tedious.

So, if they go along with the bailout, the French and Germans are in a real sense being forced to bail out their own banks via Greece. This, I believe, rather than any so-called European solidarity, will be the likely spur to any European bailout.

Other than that, Greece will have to turn to capitalism's version of the Spanish Inquisition – the IMF. It's hardly surprising that once Greece got a look at the terms the IMF was going to demand in return for IMF money the Greek government started backing away from it's earlier calls for help. Like the Inquisition, the IMF will save your soul but usually at the cost of your mortal body. 'We burn you at the stake but forgive you your sins.'

That is why we get nowhere talking loosely about 'Greece' and 'Germany'. It obscures the fact that the people of all nations are getting screwed by the financiers of every nation. Until we get that clear, we risk being set against each other like ignorant dogs much to the amusement and profit of those who created this unholy mess.

9 Apr 10

Yesterday the bond markets pushed up the rate for Greek borrowing to nearly 7.6%! This is the debt death-spiral, and the bond market knows it.

As far as I can see, there just isn't any salvation on offer for Greece. The cuts in the IMF's austerity plan would be even more draconian than the cuts involved in Germany's plan.

And there is another big problem. If, despite all their domestic political problems, Germany does go along with an EU bailout of Greece, this will give Goldman, and the other big banks and hedge funds (including German ones), a green light for taking huge bets against one country after another.

If history is anything to go by, those very bets will precipitate the crisis in borrowing costs for those countries the vultures choose to pick on. So you bet a country is likely to default and this, in itself, can increase the cost of their borrowing, which means they *are* more likely to default. Yet again, it's heads they win, tails we lose. It's quite a game for those with the money to play it.

18 Apr 10

While the banking vultures hover, as nations are plunged deeper and deeper into debt, there is an almost farcically surreal picture emerging from across the Atlantic of the moral world in which this whole crisis was incubated.

The US Securities and Exchange Commission (SEC) – the official body which describes itself as the 'investor's advocate' – is filing a lawsuit against Goldman Sachs. The SEC claims that the bank specifically created securities that were designed to fail and then knowingly sold them to pension funds and other investors claiming they were super-secure, AAA. The safest investments money can buy.

The SEC goes on to claim that Goldman then took out bets that the investments that they had designed to fail *would* fail. When they duly did, Goldman gratefully picked up their insurance payout courtesy of the taxpayers' bailout given to AIG!

If these allegations are true, it would mean that Goldman effectively got paid three times. First, for their advice to their trusting clients. Secondly, when the clients bought the securities Goldman were recommending, and thirdly, from the insurance when those very securities failed. That *would* be really smart work boys and merit very a big bonus for whoever dreamt that up.

If Goldman were to be found guilty, the case would no doubt be cited as an ugly 'bad apple' story, perpetrated by 'rogue traders'. It would be a cautionary bankers' tale used to highlight their own horror at such 'isolated' bad practice. But, if you look around, it isn't just a one-off. It's not a case of one bad apple but more like an infected orchard.

There are currently investigations into the dealings of most of the world's biggest global accountancy firms who, along with the banks they 'audit', make up the muscle and sinew of the financial world.

All the investigations point to accountants seemingly blind to the very things they are supposed to be looking for. We see mortgage brokers not properly checking on the real ability of their buyers to pay the mortgage. We see the banks and brokers securitising those loans not properly checking the real quality of those loans. We the see the banks' auditors not properly checking the banks, and we see the rating agencies not properly checking on the real quality of the securities but stamping almost anything as AAA guaranteed.

What we see are whole chains of people (and it's people we are talking about here not some faceless automated 'system') choosing to ignore the law, and their moral obligation, and instead seize their share of the rotten profit. In many cases, the bankers, their accountants, and even their regulators, are the same people who revolve from one position to another. So it's not just Goldman Sachs bankers. Not just one bad apple. Not even just one bad tree. What we see is corruption from the roots up to the very top. Any horticulturist will tell you when an orchard is infected you cannot prune or simply remove the odd tree. You have to tear every last tree out by the roots and burn the lot. I'd say this is good and sound advice.

The financial system has become systemically corrupt. It is no longer fit, or even designed, for the purpose of spreading wealth. It has become a means of looting wealth from those foolish enough to still observe the laws, and transferring it to those who regard themselves as far too clever and superior to have to bother with such trifling niceties.

19 Apr 10

Yesterday the SEC announced it had compiled a detailed complaint against Goldman Sachs. Shares across the world tumbled.

Today the SEC voted on whether or not to proceed with the case. The chairman and two democratic commissioners voted for prosecuting Goldman Sachs. The two Republican commissioners, however, voted against.

There is now a possibility the prosecution may not go ahead. Today shares in Goldman Sachs and other banks rose.

Our politicians made sure the bankers suffered no financial losses. Now, it seems, the legal world is wondering if the bankers should suffer no legal consequences either.

To my mind, if Goldman is not, at the very least, forced to answer the charges in court, then the bankers will know they can not only lose money with impunity but also act with impunity – they will truly be above the law.

What then for our futures?

CHAPTER 13

Power Grab

20 Apr 10

One of the many things I have learned over these last two years is that nothing is quite as it seems, particularly when it comes from the mouths of people with power and money. Take our friends at the IMF, who are now proposing a financial activities tax (FAT) on the banks. Is this a genuine proposal for banking reform as they claim, or does anyone smell a rat? I certainly do.

Now, I'm not against a tax, quite the contrary. I think it is a start, but only a start. The simple fact, however, is that the sums raised by the proposed IMF tax are wholly inadequate to deal with any future banking crisis as long as the current, insane leverage levels are still permitted. Every one of the major bank collapses in the US was at a bank or institution with ridiculous levels of leverage. Bear Stearns, Lehman Brothers, Fannie and Freddie, AIG, all of them, were leveraged up to their necks and beyond.

Yet the IMF says nothing about this. Neither does it say anything about breaking up the too-big-to-fail banks, or about the need to force assets to be marked-to-market and outlaw the charade of mark-to-model. It also says nothing about the critical need to regulate the credit default swap market or ban naked shorting.

That's why I don't think the tax is principally about regulating the banks at all. I think it's about the IMF grabbing new power for when another crisis does occur.

The IMF, like everybody else, knows there is a move to regulate and bail out banks internationally rather than leaving it to individual countries. I believe they want to grab as much of that power for themselves as they can. And let's remember the ability to tax *is* power. It looks like the EU may get the right to tax and create a bailout fund – I think the IMF wants the same.

As it has become bigger and increasingly powerful the EU has threatened the global hegemony of the Washington based IMF. Simply being able to say that they are the ones who regulate and deal with Europe, the world's largest trading block, has been a big smack in the face for the IMF, who are fighting back.

You can see this tension being played out over Greece. On the one hand, we have the EU saying they must be the ones to deal with Greece because it is a European country. Then we have the IMF, like a nosey neighbour, stopping by to lend a hand, sending a team to Athens anyway so that they are there in case they're needed. And, of course, as the EU has dithered so the IMF has edged its way in.

I think it is becoming clear that the IMF's desire to 'help' goes beyond friendly concern. It is, I believe, partly motivated by a fierce ideological dislike of what the IMF sees as the EU's rather more Keynesian outlook. The IMF is irrevocably on the side of those who want to bail the banks while slashing and burning public spending. The EU, for its part, is tied more closely to its member governments and is therefore open, even if only a little, to spending which supports public needs. At the end of the day both will, of course, come down on the side of the banks, but this doesn't stop them having their differences, which will come to the fore as the Greek crisis worsens.

That is why we should not be blinded to what is really going on. With their tax proposals, what I believe we are seeing is a classic power struggle over who grabs what international regulatory authority. The global elites are jostling for who gets the power over our fate next time. No one is willing to talk about really taking the obvious actions that would regulate the banks and prevent another crisis because no one wants to.

21 Apr 10

Despite the IMF's various chants and incantations aimed at restoring confidence in Greece, her position remains unchanged: default is waiting just around the corner. Yesterday, Athens had to sell at least €1.5bn in debt. It was seen as another test of Greece's ability to continue borrowing, so the fact that they sold €1.9bn has been reported as a triumph. It wasn't.

This new debt doesn't give Greece any more money. It only replaces previous short-term debt that is now maturing and needs to be repaid. The problem for Greece is that the new debt is also short-term itself, maturing in just three months. This means, in late June, Greece has to raise another €1.9bn simply to replace it.

But that isn't the end of their troubles. The rate Greece had to pay on this new debt is *double* what it paid before. So the real headline today should really be that Greece was forced to double its payments on €1.9bn of short-term debt.

The same bond buyers also made Greece pay *triple* the rate on its six-month debt, while the rate demanded on their 10-year debt is now at an all time high of 7.82%. That's 4.83% more than Germany pays.

What this all clearly says to me is that the bond buyers think Greece will pay its bill for the next three months, but after that they are not sure.

A big vote of confidence? I don't think so.

22 Apr 10

Within minutes of the markets opening this morning, Greek bonds began to sell off hard. The yield on 10-year debt shot up and a few minutes ago was at a record of 8.4%! (2pm GMT and still going up.) There is not a sinner's chance in hell that Greece can survive with debt costs that high.

This rise in interest on their future debt means that any cuts will have to be bigger and deeper than they were contemplating even yesterday. That means more unemployment, more wage cuts and a further gutting of pensions. Today it's them; tomorrow it could be us.

Earlier this week, no less a person than the German finance minister, Wolfgang Schäuble, said that if his country's citizens refused to back a joint EU-IMF bailout for Greece worth up to €45bn, they risked 'a financial meltdown'.

At the same time, Asia's newswire IGM-FX quoted 'an administrator' at the world's top investor, China's State Administration of Foreign Exchange (SAFE), who was fearful that, 'Greece could set off a chain reaction in Europe, serious enough to bring down the bigger states.'

Warnings are being voiced everywhere. So surely the Germans and the EU must bail out the Greeks, and surely the Greeks must knuckle under? Surely?

Well, 'Economic Reality', I'd like you to meet 'Political Reality'. Merkel faces elections and will be crucified if she says yes. She is trying to wait until after the election. There is a large tabloid voice in Germany much like our tabloid voice here in Britain, and, like here, politicians ignore it at their peril.

Those papers are campaigning hard against any bailout with numerous stories about lazy, profligate Greeks and headlines such as, 'You Greeks are getting nothing from us' along with articles asking, 'Why do we pay Greeks for their luxury pensions?' Of course, none of these papers are wondering what a default will do to German banks. But that would be next month's headlines. Why rush the fun and misery?

23 Apr 10

Greece finally succumbed to the pressure of the markets and literally begged for the EU–IMF bailout of €45bn.

I understand Greece needs help, but this is not the right help. It won't help the vast majority of Greek people. The bailout is effectively to help the German and French banks that are going to suffer catastrophic losses if Greece defaults. That is what this is really about: bailing out the banks in one country and yoking the people of another to pay for it. It is wrong.

The austerity programme they are planning for Greece is so punitive that it will kill off any chance of growth and recovery for the Greek people. In the end, this solution will be far more expensive and disastrous. Just look at Japan.

New research, which the previous Japanese government didn't want made public, reveals endless bank bailouts and stimulus programmes for the nonsense they are. True, Japan did not completely collapse. Its giant companies like Toyota and Sony are still giant, but there has been no prosperity for ordinary Japanese people. And that is the point. There is one economy for the elite and another for almost everyone else. According to the report, the poverty rate in Japan has doubled since the early 1990s, and most of those in work have suffered either two decades of wage stagnation or year on year wage decreases in jobs that are increasingly short-term and precarious.

Interestingly, when the new Japanese government started to spend public money to ease poverty and unemployment, suddenly the dire warnings about public spending started. Twice so far this year, the rating agencies Fitch and Moody's have 'warned' Japan that its debt level is now so large that its sovereign rating may have to be cut. They have had decades of limitless spending on banks and one failed 'stimulus' after another, and not a word is heard. We have the first signs of spending to alleviate poverty, and we get to hear insistent and immediate warnings of the need for 'fiscal consolidation'.

Does any of that sound at all familiar? Isn't this the future we are all being herded towards?

25 Apr 10

The Greeks are being told this morning, by both the EU and the IMF, that there can be no deal until they spell out the full details of their austerity plan, not only for this year but next as well. The terms must be laid out, and all parties must sign – the Greeks in their own blood.

The demands of the IMF and EU go beyond the purely economic. As part of the austerity plan the Greek people are to have certain fundamental rights taken from them, most significantly the right to collective bargaining. This is a right, remember, that they won after the overthrow of the Generals. Why must a people be told they can no longer organise themselves as they see fit? Whatever you might think of collective bargaining, isn't the power of self-determination part of what democracy was there to protect and champion?

I think the fact that the IMF and the EU want to withdraw the Greeks' right to collective bargaining, and other rights they have fought for, makes ordinary Greeks feel this is less about financial necessity and more an ideologically driven political coup.

WAKE UP PEOPLE! This is now more than economics. This is oppression coiling like a serpent round our necks.

26 Apr 10

Despite all the assurances from the IMF and the EU that Greece is going to be bailed out, reprimanded, forced to implement sweeping cuts, and made to write out, 'I shall not lie about my debt' 45 billion times, despite all that, today the interest on Greek two-year debt shot up by three percentage points to become the highest rate in the world. Greece now has to pay a whopping 13.14% on its two-year debt.

Effectively, as from today, Greece can no longer borrow. The bond market shut the door in their face and told them not to come back.

The markets are pricing in the belief that the bailout won't work, and Greece will still have to 'restructure' its debts. Restructure, in this case, means, almost but not quite, default. It means putting off paying what they owe to a later date and probably, even then, only paying back a fraction. That's why the bond market doesn't want to lend.

27 Apr 10

If all that wasn't enough, both Greek sovereign debt and Greek bank debt took another downgrade today from

Standard & Poor's. Greek financial stocks fell 17% on the news. Tomorrow, unless there is a major announcement of immediate cash guarantees, there will be more of the same. Greek banks whose vaults are stuffed with Greek national debt are cooked. They won't lend to each other. They can't borrow at any rate that they can afford, and now their central bank is broke. If there isn't a bank run in the next few days, I'll be amazed. (Then again, I have often been amazed by events of these last two years.)

Greece needs Germany, in particular, to fork out NOW. But, while the Greeks need immediate action, the Germans have to pass a bill to allow them to bail Greece out. Time is against them both.

I think debt restructuring must now be a very real possibility. The bond market certainly thinks so. Who hedged against default and who didn't is the question that matters. My money is on Deutsche reaping big credit default swap rewards and Commerzbank and Société Générale the big losers. We'll see.

The uncertainty is having repercussions everywhere. In stocks, volatility indexes are shooting up with the bond troubles creating considerable market turbulence. And turbulence, as any mathematician will tell you, is unpredictable and dangerous stuff to mess with. This, I think, is the crux of the matter: markets never seem to grasp the nature of their own non-linearity.

In linear systems the past predicts the future. Changes of direction are smooth and step wise. The next step is just like the last and continues a trend, up or down, in a predictable fashion. In the non-linear world none of this holds true. Change is abrupt and goes in lurches, bumps, drops and U-turns.

Yesterday, the bond markets were liquid and flush. Today, worry takes hold, and suddenly traders see what they saw yesterday in a very different light. This surfacing of worry itself breeds more worry. Maybe debt will be harder to sell with buyers scarcer and less willing to take risks.

If so, then countries like Portugal, Spain, Ireland and Italy might find themselves competing for buyers. So Portugal is bobbing along, but suddenly, today, she gets a two-notch downgrade of her sovereign debt. That means she's on the last and bottom rung of the A range. The next drop is into B territory. Not only was Portugal downgraded, but there was suddenly a significant spike in worry over Spanish, Italian and Irish debts.

Italy has been seen as doing amazingly well, so far. Until now, no one seemed to think it worth worrying why and how. Suddenly, their last bond auction barely got enough bids to sell the debt on offer. That, in itself, caused people who had not worried to start asking questions. 'Can Italy really be doing this well? Might there be liabilities they are hiding?' Once that worry takes hold things can change very quickly.

I believe we might be at one of those moments when, rather suddenly, what everyone saw as reassuringly half-full seems to be worryingly half-empty. Markets are always taken by surprise by such moments.

With this shift in sentiment, the credit default swap market now looks like it may even turn to Germany. There are even whispers about Germany's credit rating being looked at – expressed in the most whispered tones you understand. I think Merkel knows this and is weighing up her options. Which way does Germany get screwed most? If they don't bail out Greece, maybe German banks take large hits and have to be bailed out themselves. On the other hand, if they do bail Greece out, they may have to watch as the costs of their own debt go up.

Why would they go up? Well, the markets will start to bet that Germany will be forced into helping Portugal and then others in turn. How sure can the market be that Portugal would need help? Well, fairly sure, because the market can make it happen. And they will, because that is how they intend to make their next killing.

The big banks in every country are fighting for their own survival. They have large losses still accruing. They need to make large profits very quickly. They will NOT do this through 'lending to small and medium businesses to promote recovery'. That is just political prole-fodder, catnip for the masses. The banks have to make the kind of profits that they can ONLY make by speculating on large moves. Luckily for them (Mammon be praised!) they can help make those moves happen. All you need is instability. Lots of worries to move the cost one way, and lots of government interventions and assurances to move it back. It's that simple. Insecurity is profit.

And therein lies the opportunity for another killing. Push Portuguese debt levels up. Create a panic. Bet on another bailout, and feel the pleasure when your bets are covered, yet again, by the whimpering politicians.

Portugal, Spain and then Italy can all be pushed nearer the edge because the banks and hedge funds can potentially make billions doing it. Of course, it is a dangerous and ultimately destructive game of speculation that often kills the debtor. But it is lucrative, and it is the only way to make the kinds of profits the big banks need to survive.

How all of this unfolds, and whether there is any knock on effect on Spain or Portugal, depends on who makes what profit from a Greek default. If it works in Greece, it will work again. That will be the conclusion. Then they will be keen to play the game with Portugal and Spain. If the profits are too slim, because there are no government back ups for empty credit default swap contracts, then they won't be so keen to try it again.

All of which would make you think Germany would be mad to bail out Greece. But if they don't, German, French and Swiss banks take a big hit almost straight away with all the fallout that will entail.

Anyone remember when Bernanke said that 'subprime was contained'?

29 Apr 10

One of the main reasons that the problem won't be contained is because of the amount of short-term debt now in the system.

As I have been pointing out for a while, the first thing many governments did when they started having problems was to start to sell short-term debt instead of long-term debt. It is easier to get buyers and generally cost less. The downside is that it also makes your overall situation much more unsteady. That's because the more short-term debt you have, the more often you have to keep coming back to the markets. Long-term debt is done, out of the way, and the money is yours for a decade or more. Short-term debt is like having to sign on the dole every week. It takes time, makes you feel bad, and every time you worry they'll say NO. Not this week.

France, Italy and Spain all have a lot of short-term debt that has to be rolled over. France has €281bn, Italy has €240bn and Spain has €100bn. All this means plenty of instability and chances for someone to come up short with a no-bid auction.

The other reason the problem won't be contained to Greece alone is growth, or, should I say, the lack of it. Just look at Spain again. Standard & Poor's (S&P) downgraded the country's credit rating yesterday. This took everyone by surprise, not least the Spanish themselves. Spain has less debt than Greece and more earning power than Portugal, so why the downgrade?

The reason, according to a report by S&P quoted in yesterday's Wall Street Journal, was because: 'We now believe that the Spanish economy's shift away from credit-fuelled economic growth is likely to result in a more protracted period of sluggish activity than we previously assumed.'

This is bad news, according to S&P, because without debt-fuel Spain won't grow fast enough to offset problems that include: 'private sector indebtedness, high unemployment, a fairly low export capacity, and an unwinding of the government's fiscal stimulus to reduce general government deficit.'

If the rating agencies are getting worried that growth is likely to be too slow to deal with all the mounting problems, then this will set alarm bells ringing in a lot of national treasuries. What, for example, are the UK's prospects for growth?

From the figures coming in, it seems quite clear that we will *not* get sufficiently large or rapid enough growth to make any significant difference to our debt problems. That's why the UK's first credit rating downgrade will happen. Not just because of large debts, nor a hung parliament, but because we can't point to any prospect of good growth.

That's a big problem for the politicians. Obviously every party prefers to preside over growth and announce policies for promoting it rather than being the party of cuts and tax rises. The reality they will have to face, however, is that if growth doesn't take place at anything like the rate needed, then the government, of whatever party, will have to cut spending AND increase taxes. The problem is made worse by the fact that, without a significant recovery and growth in the real economy, unemployment will stay high. This will further cripple any hope of decent tax revenues meaning any spending cuts will have to be even deeper.

As for taxing the rich, can you imagine any of the parties seriously threatening to do that? To tax the rich, and close all their loopholes and avoidance schemes, would, we will no doubt be told, 'threaten the recovery'. In this world, we all have to hope the rich get richer and not do anything that might 'jeopardise wealth creation'. It's us, not the wealthy, who will have to pay.

This means benefits and unemployment pay will be first in line to get cut. The parties will differ on how hard to chop, but chop they will – with regret in one case and glee in the other. Then there will have to be long-term savings, which means only one thing: public sector pensions. The government assault will be like a high-speed train. If you're a public sector worker caught at the crossing, unless you can derail the train first, they will have to identify you by your dental records.

So Brown and Cameron can argue about how much public spending should be cut and how quickly, but these differences are akin to the differences between First World War generals. They all agreed on slaughtering the grunts in the trenches but just differed over the time and place of carnage.

That, however, won't be the end of our indignity. While we are suffering cuts to our services and living standards the bankers will be telling those in power that only they can save the country from stagnation and downgrade! The banks will tell whoever is elected that speculation is freedom, leverage is salvation and regulation is the road to perdition. In public, they will attempt to dress themselves in the garb of national saviours. In private, they will piss themselves laughing at us and our pathetic political leaders.

That's why we need to wake up to what is happening. In 1979, we were told the problem was the big bad unions and that we should vote for the person who was going to give them a good kicking. We did. (That's the generalised 'we', not me, so please no shouting.)

This time the problem is the bankers, but no one is saying they are going to give the bankers a kicking. Oh no! They may be the problem, but we are assured they are the only ones who can save us. And the way they save us is by the magic of them getting rich first, and then, at some unspecified date, brushing a few crumbs down to everyone below

And that won't be all. If the government doesn't follow their commands, they will begin to act. There will be 'pressure from the bond market' about our debt. At least that is how it will be generally reported. In reality, it will be something quite different. It will be pressure created *on* the bond market *by* investment banks and others speculating on the cost of insuring UK debt using credit default swaps. They won't be doing this because they have any debt they are worried about. They will be doing it because it is a great way of making profits. That's how the cost of insuring our debt will be ramped up. And when it is, the bond market will start demanding higher interest rates on our debt, which will mean yet more spending cuts to pay for it. And, guess what? The banks will be doing all this speculating against us with the bailout cash that we gave them.

This is the deadly irony of the situation all our governments have got us into. The result was as entirely predictable as it is tragic.

CHAPTER 14

All Our Futures

1 May 10

From the very start of this crisis I have lamented the fact that there was never any real debate about nature of the crisis. Was it a crisis of liquidity or solvency? Should the banks be bailed out, or should they be forced to pay off their bad debts and go bankrupt if necessary? Should we incur vast public debt on their behalf or not? These were fundamental questions that were never properly debated.

I understand the crisis was fast moving, but not *that* fast and not all the time. There were long periods when a proper political and public debate could have taken place. What happened instead was that we were subjected to a chorus of hectoring voices from the financial class, backed up by their slavering politicians and lapdog journalists. They all shared, it seemed to me, one common purpose: to prevent any real debate about what needed to be done. At one of the most critical periods in recent history, our democracy seriously failed us. We are all living with the consequences of that failure.

One compelling piece of evidence demonstrating how that debate was actually stifled came yesterday in transcripts just released of the Fed meeting held on March 16, 2004.

At that meeting, they were discussing fears of a possible housing bubble developing. The president of the Atlanta Federal Reserve, Jack Guynn, explained the situation: 'A number of folks are expressing growing concern about potential overbuilding and worrisome speculation in the real estate markets, especially in Florida, with buyers freely admitting that they have no intention of occupying the units or building on the land but rather are counting on "flipping" the properties – selling them quickly at higher prices.'

A suggestion was made to lay out the facts of the developing housing bubble in a public document to stimulate discussion and debate.

The Fed chairman at the time, no other than Alan Greenspan, made it crystal clear what he thought: 'We run the risk,' he said, 'by laying out the pros and cons of a particular argument, of inducing people to join in on the debate, and in this regard it is possible to lose control of a process that only we fully understand.'

There it is. Read it again!

There could be no clearer statement of contempt for you as a thinking adult. No clearer admission that control was the only priority. Informed debate was strangled and in its place came assurances that 'what had to be done' was being done by those educated and expert enough to do it. You, little people, just pipe down and remember your place. Speak when spoken to, and do what you're told.

That was in 2004, when the crisis was being incubated. Do you really think the attitude of those in power changed when the folly of their actions became apparent?

There was no debate, and there still isn't, because those in power would rather your children grew up without hope of a job, without hope of a career, without hope of a decent education or a national health service, as long as their financial system and their wealth remains. They would rather all that than allow you any real debate or choice.

Had we had a proper debate at the beginning, we might have at least heard the arguments against bailing out the banks and taking on such debt. But, now that we have incurred those debts, can you imagine being allowed to even think about changing course? When the banks ask for more of our money, will there be any debate about it? Would we even be allowed to debate repudiating the debts taken so far?

It seems to me that when it comes to finance we can chose any party, any course of action we like, so long as it falls within a narrow range of 'acceptable choices' and never threatens the control of those who claim to know what's best.

All this makes me wonder whether we still live in a real democracy. Or are we just living in a pretend one? One in which we get to dress up in its clothes, and speak its language, but where it is stripped of its real, meaningful and radical content.

3 May 10

For all their lies, bluster and arrogance our leaders are now clearly panicking and desperate.

We got a sign of that at the weekend when the European Central Bank (ECB) finally surrendered its last vestige of prudence. Back in January, the bank had said they wouldn't debase their lending rules or their credibility any further. They have just done both.

At a critical moment in the crisis, the markets and the ECB stood toe to toe and looked for weakness. Unsurprisingly, the ECB blinked first and agreed to accept any Greek bonds the banks wanted to unload. As from now, the ECB will loan

Greek banks, and anyone else's banks, brand new euros in return for virtually worthless Greek bonds. These are bonds that will either default in the next six months or take a better part of a decade to regain their value. It was a test, and the ECB failed. The market now knows who's the alpha and who's the cur.

Call it what you want: it's a bailout in all but name.

Those who made the decision will no doubt say that in such an emergency there is nothing else they could have done. If they had cut Greek banks off from ECB borrowing, the banks would have collapsed and so would Greece. That is true. No one else will accept the stuff for any meaningful amount. If they would, it could be bought and traded on the open market. It's not. The tragedy is that in being the one who exchanges real cash for bits of Greek paper, the ECB itself now becomes a bank with worthless assets and huge unsupported lending.

Back in 2008, the big banks were in that situation. We saved them by moving the problem up to the level of nations. Now nations are in the same trouble, and we are moving the lies and pretence up another level. The ECB becomes the latest hiding place of bank and now sovereign debts.

It's the same situation in the US. The Fed now has a balance sheet of over a trillion dollars of stuff now worth a fraction of what they paid for it. Where do we hide the problem next? The great big bank in the sky?

You might have thought, that by opening herself to all the Greek crap held by the banks, the ECB action would have steadied the markets. It didn't. Instead we got a dip. Could the dip be the sign of a real shift in sentiment and the beginning of a much bigger drop? I am not sure. I don't think so, not quite yet.

As long as enough Greeks and Germans alike believe that the austerity measures will work and pull Greece back to solvency then both groups will grin and bear it. If that is the case, the markets may avoid a big, immediate fall. The problem arises if enough ordinary Greeks think the plan isn't going to work and believe they will be made to suffer for richer people's profit. Then, quite understandably and quite rationally, they will take to the streets and withhold their cooperation. That will change things. In those circumstances, unless the Greek government are willing to order their police to shed their own people's blood, they won't be able to carry through the necessary cuts.

If the Greeks do decide that they are not going to go meekly to the slaughter – for economic slaughter it will most assuredly be – then the Germans will almost certainly back out. Why commit money to a project that will burn the cash and still fail? I think the best the German politicians will do is promise to open the taps, but make sure they can shut them down at a moment's notice.

Such a compromise will most certainly *not* work for the bond market and risks making the fear of failure self-fulfilling. That is the logic being turned over in the minds of bond buyers. It is why PIMCO doesn't believe the crisis is over. I agree.

The markets are also looking beyond Greece. Spanish banks, in particular, have been taking a hammering. In part, I think this is because the market suspects that some of the Spanish banks, and also their regional savings institutions, the *Cajas,* are in real difficulty.

The Spanish government itself isn't in a much better situation. Increasing national debt and insurance costs are starting to hurt. Their bonds are like dynamite. If they start to sweat as debt servicing costs heat up, then BOOM. I think the Spanish are hoping the ECB will step in like the Fed has done in the

US. The problem is the ECB isn't the Fed. It doesn't have the might of the US Treasury behind it. If the ECB tries to act like the Fed, it will end up like the French at Agincourt: all pomp and pride, ending in blood and shame.

What was that someone said about recovery?

4 May 10

Despite all the mayhem in Europe it is still important to keep an eye on China.

Last week the Chinese government outlawed lending for *third* homes. To have to legislate against lending for third homes tells us this is a real verruca of a problem. So far they have tried to either dig or burn it out, but it is so big and recalcitrant it seems like they are now going to try and freeze it.

The problem the Chinese have is that property isn't being bought by people who want to live in it but by people who either want to sell it on for a quick profit or hold it while it goes up in value. There are now tens of millions of square metres of empty, unused property space throughout China. The parallels with the US housing bubble that precipitated this whole crisis haven't gone unnoticed. Speculation makes paper profits. But, as we all now know, paper can quickly catch fire and turn to ash.

The Chinese central authorities are trying desperately to shut off the speculation before it does turn to flames. The government wants, and needs, to have sustainable investment in production. The problem is that as they try to rein back speculation, investors are getting worried. If property speculation is damped down then a reduction in new building will follow. The elephant in the ointment is that up to 60% of China's economy is tied to the construction industry.

Just take concrete. China now produces over 40% of the entire world's concrete to feed this building boom. That means mining companies make a fortune digging up the raw materials and coal and power companies make a fortune meeting the gargantuan appetite concrete production has for power. It's therefore not such a great leap of the imagination to see how a serious contraction in the property market could easily lead to a severe slow down in the rest of the economy and even a crash.

There are some who think that growth elsewhere will offset any losses when China's property bubble deflates. I think they will be proved wrong.

China has a bubble, and it is not going to deflate gently: it's going to burst. When it does, it will take a lot of the property speculators, large and small, with it. People with three or twenty-three properties, which they believe are 'better than money in the bank', will eventually find their paper worth starting to evaporate. Their 'money' will be gone. Along with them, the whole chain, from mining and energy companies to indebted and leveraged builders, will feel the pain.

Repeat after me: China is not going to save us; China is not going to save us.

5 May 10

Today looks like the day when the fun really starts. This morning, while the IMF was proudly puffing on its announcement that it would agree the plan and loan for Greece, the Greek people and the bond market had other ideas.

The Greek people went for the general strike and occupation of the Acropolis option. The bond market, for their part, decided to play for keeps. Credit default swaps on all the so-called PIIGS (Portugal, Ireland, Italy, Greece, Spain) exploded this morning.

The bond market will not believe in any bailout so long as there is the possibility that the people, at some point, could turn around and throw the deal, and the government who made it, out the window. And that is the problem for the EU and the IMF. In a word – people. They are a problem. They sometimes just won't do what their betters require. THANK GOD!

The fear of contagion is not financial contagion or debt contagion – those fears have already taken hold. The real contagion the financial class are terrified of is political contagion: the fear that the people of other countries will follow the lead of the Greeks in fighting back against the cuts being imposed on them.

In my opinion, the Greek people are doing exactly the right thing. No one asked them if they liked the deal being offered. The IMF, the EU and their own government have simply struck a deal which suits them and addresses their worries but assigns the costs and pain to the majority of Greek people.

Why should ordinary people just passively agree to be shafted by the IMF, the EU, Greek banks and the wealthy class of Greeks who will pay nothing towards the pain of this bailout? Why should they agree?

I don't think they should. I think they should do what they are doing. They should play hardball. They should bargain in a way their own government was too chicken shit scared to do or, more likely, didn't really want to do because their loyalties aren't actually with their own people but with the bankers.

The fact is that the EU and the big European banks need this deal more than the Greek people do. That is the hand the Greeks have to play. They should play it to the end. Ordinary Greeks will not be even worse off if Greece defaults. The rich will be. The banks will be. The former bank executives in key positions in the Greek government will be. But the bulk of people in Greece will not be.

If the Greek people hold out, the IMF, and certainly the EU, will have to either accept a colossal default and collapse of many banks, or they will have to come back to the Greek people with better terms.

The French, German and Swiss banks have over a hundred billion euros worth of Greek debt alone. They all have even more Spanish debt. The Brits are rolling in it. Then there are all the other countries in the EU with debt problems. As fears of sovereign default or debt restructuring grow so the worth of all those bonds goes down. This has nasty side effects for the banks.

Any banks holding that sovereign debt suddenly become worth less than they were because what they hold has lost value. This means their share prices go down, their capital holdings shrink, and they may have to think about raising more capital. Bailout anyone?

But that's not all. Because banks count sovereign debt as capital, they all use it as collateral when they lend to each other. If the value of that debt goes down then so does everyone's willingness to accept it as collateral – at least not for long, and not without charging a hefty premium.

And that is what is starting to happen. Just like when the credit crunch began two years ago, banks are now beginning to charge each other higher and higher rates to borrow for any longer than just overnight. Three-month lending is still happening, but it's getting more and more expensive.

No country need actually default for one or more of the banks holding a lot of sovereign debt to find borrowing in the markets impossible or too expensive. If that happens, and one or more of the banks go down, there is then the risk it could start a domino effect among other banks, just as Lehmans did.

Let that thought sink in for a minute.

Two years on, hundreds and hundreds of billions of pounds later (trillions if you included the US bailouts) and nothing, precisely NOTHING has changed … except one thing: the problem of the original bad debts has now got bigger, MUCH BIGGER. Now, instead of just banks, we have whole countries facing collapse as well. This is where the insane policy of bailing out the banks' bad debts has led us.

Nothing has changed because, as some of us have argued from the very beginning, nothing was ever done about the bad debts in the first place. The bad debts didn't go away. Our governments simply took them from the banks and willingly wheeled them into the national vault for them to poison the finances there. But this isn't a disease that can be quarantined. Now the problems caused by those debts at the sovereign level are working their way back down to the banks again.

And the banks' solution to this? Easy. Not content with ruining whole countries, why not try and destroy a whole continent. Let's wheel the infected paper to an even bigger vault, the ECB's, and let it rot there.

And that, of course, is what our supine politicians have started to do in accepting practically worthless Greek bonds from the banks. They are acquiescing, yet again, to the bankers' demands, no matter what the cost. Have they learnt nothing at all from the last two years? Are they so spineless and lacking in moral conviction that there is nothing they wouldn't do to protect the rich and the wealthy at the expense of their own people?

Sadly, we all know the answer. Our leaders have chosen the path of not clearing any bad debts but of supporting those who made them. Having thrown vast sums into this policy, it was obvious that possible failure would create a huge pressure to keep on doing it because to stop would be to admit the failure of an idiotic first decision. And so it is playing out.

6 May 10

The fear that Greece might not be contained was enough to knock the Dow down 800 points this morning with the financial sector hit hardest. It is rallying now, but you can bet that is pure intervention. They have been jokingly dubbed the PPT or Plunge Protection Team – the financial world's Men in Black – the last line of defence. They are, of course, no more than some of the primary dealers using their own or the Fed's cash to intervene and stop market sentiment from doing too much damage. It's now back to 'only' a 350 point drop.

The important thing, however, isn't how much the market fell, or how much it claws back. The point is that it shows financial stocks, particularly, are very fragile. It also demonstrates that the system of which they are a part is so unstable that a worry, just a worry that one country might default, is enough to send them all, like lemmings, over a cliff. This plunge gives the lie to the party line that everything has been dealt with and contained.

If they were all healthy, well-capitalised and their assets were really worth what they claim they are worth, then their stocks would not have plunged. But they did. Whatever they might like us to think, the fact is that the banks are still lying about their assets and still hiding bad debts. They are also still using levels of leverage that are inherently unstable. They are so unstable that they used to be illegal for that very reason. Now, with the threat of sovereign defaults, they are suddenly exposed to even greater losses, and with those levels of leverage even quite small defaults threaten to wipe out whole swathes from their balance sheets. All the bankers know this; all the dealers know this. That's why the entire ship started to roll.

And they've got worse to come. Spain is starting to worry some people a lot more than Greece. The interest it has to pay on its debt has risen from 2.8% in March to 3.5% today. When you are talking billions of euros that is NOT a small revision. But it's not just the amount they have to pay on their debt that is causing the problems. Spain admitted today that most of its regional savings and loans institutions, the *Cajas*, which make up about half of Spain's financial system, are so badly exposed to the property crisis that they will have to be bailed out, restructured or merged if many of them aren't to collapse.

This combination of a sovereign debt crisis and the failure of many *Cajas* could certainly push Spain to where Greece is now. That is starting to cause panic in the bond markets. If Spain were to default on its debts, that would be the equivalent of Chernobyl compared to a Greek Three Mile Island.

In the face of this, 'a noted investment strategist' quoted by Marketwatch said he felt that, by its actions, the market was telling Jean-Claude Trichet, head of the ECB, '... to get your act together and provide some leadership and establish some order.'

Of course, what he means by that is BAIL US OUT! Buy all the rotten and worthless Greek, Spanish and other debts that we no longer want. We don't care what it costs you or what bad things it does to anyone else at any point in the future. Just make sure we, and all the people we do business with, don't face any losses. That's what – imperiously dressing it up in pompous exhortations to provide leadership – he is rabidly barking in our faces.

This 'noted investment strategist' knows the danger that awaits, and he wants something done about it. Not the right thing; not the thing that might help all us little people. No. Something specifically designed to help him and those who are in the same financial quick sand he is in.

If the bond market seizes up because of the fear of sovereign defaults, lots of bondholders will first lose their expensively tailored shirts and then their minds. That's what he's indignant about. Not whether Monsieur Trichet is showing proper leadership. The bond market lent unwisely. They hoped to make money. Now they won't. But they want you to believe it's nothing to do with them: it's just bad leadership by a central bank that won't bend over.

7 May 10

The rout continues:

London down 3.2% – 170 points
Tokyo down 3.1% – 330 points
Frankfurt down 3.2% – 193 points
Paris down 4.6% – 164 points
Dow down 1.77% -187 points

Losses everywhere are not only continuing but accelerating. They'll pull back in late trading no doubt. But confidence? I don't think so.

Yesterday the New York Stock Exchange tried to tell the world that the collapse was due to a 'rogue trader' who punched in the wrong figures on a trade. Someone ought to arrest that fool soon. That must be the third or fourth time he's screwed things up for everyone else!

Fat finger or not, bank stocks everywhere are seriously hurting. And that is *with* the German parliament agreeing to the bailout. If the challenge to the bailout in the German courts holds things up then Greece is definitely cooked. If it doesn't, it's just a matter of time. Whatever happens it looks like Merkel is going to pay the price in the regional elections.

The UK, for its part, is going to get hammered when it becomes clear that there isn't a working parliamentary majority to jump when the market says so. I think the FTSE is headed under 5000. The Dow is under 10k. The Nikkei is in trouble. This could be the start of something big.

Some very interesting news is just coming through. Remember yesterday when the 'noted investment strategist' demanded that Monsieur Trichet and the ECB 'show some leadership'? Well, it looks like he might be getting his way. There is a rumour going around that this weekend the ECB will announce a €600bn bailout package! Such expensive rumours are cheap to spread. Let's see what happens.

8 May 10

The EU leaders met and today confirmed they are going to set up a new fund to 'defend the euro at all costs.'

Oh dear, our politicians still think this is about saving the euro. In fairness, I am sure that's what many bankers and financial experts are telling him. The sad fact is that if they 'defend' the euro 'at all costs' then that is exactly what it will cost them: everything. The EU just gave the banks and speculators the signal: bet against us and eventually you will do for the euro what Soros did to the pound.

If this bailout goes ahead on Monday, bank shares will lift and the markets will rally. Our wonderful experts and leaders will beam with pride. Then slowly reality will draw tighter, inch-by-inch, around their necks. Debt costs will grow after a brief respite. So will the cost of insuring that debt. Portugal, Spain and Italy will slide back into trouble.

So far none of the bailouts have worked; this one won't either. Debt – unpaid, undeclared, unaddressed – is the problem. Borrowing more to hide it doesn't solve the problem: it just makes it bigger. We may not have a meltdown for a few months yet, but a meltdown is coming.

10 May 10

It is official. The bailout is back and bigger than ever. Do you know what you can buy with SEVEN HUNDRED AND FIFTY BILLION EUROS? You can buy an immediate 4.5% rise on the FTSE and an immediate 4% rise on the Dow. You also can get 29 of 30 stocks on the Dow to go up,

Hurrah all is saved! Or is it?

Take a look at the euro. Friday it hit its low of 1.26 to the dollar. Its year high was 1.52. After we said that our plan for saving the economy was that we were going to borrow €750bn, the euro went up to 1.31 for a few hours. Then it began to drop all the way back to 1.28 where it is now. Two cents from its low point. Bravo!

So, while the stock markets cheered – for the moment – the currency markets and bond markets are waiting. Waiting to see if governments force the austerity measures upon their people with an iron fist. If not, then the euro is going to sink further.

One leading economist from Morgan Stanley, reported today, made the bankers' view extremely clear: 'If the emergency liquidity for the periphery is not complemented by aggressive austerity measures, the underlying solvency problems could continue to fester and eventually spread to the core.'

I am sorely tempted to hit this man.

The banks have had 'underlying solvency problems' for two years, but not one word has been said by the banking experts about that. Oh, no! That's just talked of as 'liquidity problem'. For the bankers, it's only the public who have solvency problems. And now the banks have loaded their debts on to us, again, those debts mustn't be allowed to fester. *We* must be subjected to 'aggressive austerity measures'. Not the banks. No. No austerity for them at all. Quite the opposite in fact.

As for his fear that it might spread to 'the core'. You might think he means Germany and France. Wrong. He means the big banks. How do I know that? Because it is the big banks who are exposed to the debts. If Greece, Portugal or Spain had defaulted, Germany wouldn't have fallen, but some of its banks might. At least one French bank would certainly have gone down. Would French people or French culture have died? I think not.

In bankers' minds, the banks are the 'core', while we, the people and our national life, are merely 'the periphery'. We got a similar message from one of the leading lights at Société Générale: 'Without fiscal consolidation', he told us, 'all of this is for naught because public sector finances in many states are unsustainable and need to be consolidated.'

Translated this reads: 'Having saddled public finances with our debts we must now get people to forget that and insist that prudence and a belief in sound economic management mean that your governments must now eviscerate all other parts of public spending, for the common good, of course.' This from a bank who could have sunk without our bailout being given to Greece!

This bailout was never about clearing up after 'lazy and profligate southern Europeans.' That story is to distract your attention from the fact that this bailout is for the banks, AGAIN. That is what it has always been about. Do you think this money would have been made available if it was simply the people of Greece or Spain who needed it and not the banks? Of course not. We are simply the Tommies to be sent to slaughter to make good on the General's big push.

11 May 10

Today that €750bn masterstroke of financial genius has been revealed for what it was.

The debasement of the euro bought nothing more than staving off the inevitable. Nothing was solved. Not one of the fundamental issues was addressed.

Yesterday saw a 10% rise in Paris. Today 1.5% of it has gone already. London had a 5% rise yesterday and a 1% fall today. If the bailout had been the solution to the fundamental problems, addressing the root causes of our crisis, there would be no drop today because everyone would have known that we had tackled the cause of the disease. But we didn't. And the markets know that. They know today, as they knew yesterday, that the actions our leaders took, while they made bankers richer, left us in the same mess we were in before, only mired even deeper.

I am not saying we won't see slow gains. We may well do. But the dawn of a new, clean 'mission accomplished' financial era? No. The net result of this folly is that we now have €750bn less for dealing with the real issues and events that are still going to unfold. And unfold they will.

The financial class know this. They may be the lowest form of human life, but when it comes to defending their wealth they are not stupid. They know they need to make us, not them, pay for those debts whatever it costs. That's why, to quote one leading market analyst, 'there are still doubts on whether the peripheral countries can deliver on austerity.' That's their worry now. That is what the financial class sees as the proper and apparently only role of government. DELIVER ON AUSTERITY. That is what your government is for. Welcome to your future.

There is now no easy way out of the killing field we have been led into. And it must be becoming clear to people that a killing field is a good description of the place they are taking us.

Men in fine suits, with fine degrees, who live golden lives, have led us and our children to a desperate place. Our political leaders have helped them take us there. They chose not to spend our future taxes on education, on health, on investment in a better future, but instead they sacrificed it all to save the banks. That sacrifice will involve tearing from us every thread in the fabric of our national life that is not tied down and defended tooth and nail. It is the ultimate failure of imagination and courage by a generation of political leaders.

The pain they have stored up for us will not go away. This means, in my opinion, there are only two futures remaining for us. One is where the pain comes quickly in which we do everything to make sure it is the financial class, and not us, who suffer the most. But there is another future, the one they have planned for us, where it happens slowly, the pain getting greater and greater with time, but where it is made to fall on us rather than the immensely rich people and institutions that caused the crisis.

It is the future where everything we have sacrificed and struggled to build to make this country a better place – our universities, our schools, our pensions, our health service – is hacked down and the little left is subjected to the laws and logic of the market, where nothing is valued but profit.

That is the future they want; it is the future we must resist, and it is a future we have to confront together or each of us will be pulverized by it on our own.

With that future in mind our political leaders know everything now is about enforcement – about enforcing this future upon us. In simple terms it means what we are seeing in Greece, and what we saw in Iceland. It means police versus people. It is where Democracy and Finance run into each other like bulls in a field. It will come here too.

If you believe, like me, that the only long-term and sustainable path out of the killing fields we have been led to is for the ordinary people of all countries to force the bad debts to be taken by those who made them, and put an end to public money being misused to bail out the wealthy, then we must act now. The longer we delay, the longer we put off the inevitable, the greater the pain for all of us.

In my opinion democracy – when you have it already – is about peaceful voting. When you don't have it, or you are in danger of having it hollowed out so that what remains serves only the rich and the powerful, then it is time for standing up and confronting those who would deny you. That time is now. Our political leaders, if we let them, will deliver us to the killing fields. A different leadership will have to come from the bottom, from you and me, to stop them.

Acknowledgements

The first and foremost person I would like to thank is my friend and colleague, Mark Tanner.

Some people write books. I had mine thrust upon me – by Mark. All I did was write furious comments on the Guardian website and then on my own blog. It was Mark who had the vision and determination to take hundreds of pages of outrage and turn them into the book you have in your hands. Without him there would simply be no book. So if there is someone you want to blame, blame him. I do.

I know Mark, for his part, would especially like to thank Lucy Frith for her invaluable comments on earlier drafts as well as also thanking David Frith, Susan Tanner and David Green for their advice and suggestions. He would also like to thank Adam Gac for being able to weather yet another storm and Cristina Odone for all her help and advice. I too would like to thank them.

I would also like to acknowledge Karl Denninger and many of the other people who posted comments at the tickerforum. org. Karl's clear, if abrasive, writings on financial matters were, and continue to be, an education. So too are the thoughts and postings of those who run and contribute to zerohedge. com. These two websites are where I most frequently went to learn and question the prevailing wisdom.

Along with those two sites, I am indebted to the community of people who have regularly contributed thoughts and insights on the financial pages of the Guardian. Some of these people must share some of the blame for encouraging me to start a blog. (As if the world really needed another.) Many of those people are now part of the community who contribute to the blog. My thanks to all of you. Anyone who wants to put names to the guilty parties need only visit the blog to find them at work.

In addition, I would like to thank Paul Ormerod for writing The Death of Economics, which did exactly what it said on the tin.

In terms of the actual physical production of the book, along with the help I received from James Malone, my thanks go to Duncan Beal, Cathi Poole, Paula Charles and Clare Brayshaw at York Publishing Services who have made the process of getting into print as easy and as painless as possible.

Lastly, I would like to thank Sara Fenander who is, for me, the reason why.

INDEX